A
Psychonaut's Guide
to the
Invisible Landscape

The Topography of the
Psychedelic Experience

Dan Carpenter

Park Street Press
Rochester, Vermont

Park Street Press
One Park Street
Rochester, Vermont 05767
www.InnerTraditions.com

Park Street Press is a division of Inner Traditions International

LIBRARY OF CONGRESS CATALOGING-IN-PUBLICATION DATA
Carpenter, Dan, 1963–2005
  A psychonaut's guide to the invisible landscape : the topography of the psychedelic
experience / Dan Carpenter.
    p. cm.
  Includes bibliographical references.
  ISBN 1-59477-090-5 (pbk.)
  1. Hallucinogenic drugs—Psychological aspects. 2. Hallucinogenic drugs and
religious experience. 3. Consciousness. 4. Carpenter, Dan, 1963–2005 I. Title.
  BF209.H34C37 2006
  154.4—dc22

                                                    2005033548

Printed and bound in the United States by Lake Book Manufacturing, Inc.

10 9 8 7 6 5 4 3 2 1

Text design and layout by Virginia Scott Bowman
This book was typeset in Life and Myriad with Rockwell as the display typeface

Contents

✳

Acknowledgments

Thank you Beth Gallagher, who put up with my oddities and who shared many a laugh with me.

To my parents Fran and Carol Carpenter, for helping me in the lean days and for having me! (And for letting me use their computer.)

To Melissa Yates for her love and support.

To the reader . . . thank you for your interest . . . enjoy.

Foreword

We don't know when humans first began to use consciousness-changing substances to explore their interior landscapes. It may go back to the origin of our species, perhaps well before that. Some scholars theorize that early munching of psychedelic plants and fungi might have helped to catalyze a quantum leap in mental development, leading to language, perhaps, as well as the first artistic expressions of communion with the sacred, scratched out on cave walls. We do know that the modern West turned against archaic traditions of witchcraft and shamanism with the Inquisition, beginning a practice of repressing individual investigation of altered states that has continued, through the "War on Drugs," to the present day.

Although they are no longer burnt at the stake for their efforts, those who have tried to reclaim this area as a legitimate one for human inquiry still confront serious obstacles. Despite early masterpieces of drug literature by Thomas de Quincy, Samuel Coleridge, and others, and an intellectual interest in this area stretching from the Romantic poets through the Surrealists, the mainstream of the West has centered on empirical science and technological progress, with its presumed objectivity and bias against subjective experience. The materialist perspective, obsessed with fact and linear logic, has tended to dismiss the individual investigation of consciousness as unimportant, even disreputable. The mainstream paradigm was given a severe but short-lived shake during the psychedelic upsurge of the 1960s—led by intellectuals such as Aldous Huxley, Alan Watts, Allen Ginsberg, Timothy Leary, and others—who advocated substance-based exploration of the mind as a tool for self-discovery and deconditioning from the proscribed codes of a mass-mediated society. The gnostic upsurge of the 1960s collapsed into societal chaos and new forms of repression, and the inspiration went underground again, surfacing in movies and music, given mischievous expression by the psychedelic theorist Terence McKenna, who kept the flame alive during the 1980s and 1990s.

As the historian Michel Foucault has noted, repression leads to dispersion and proliferation of discourses. The governmental fatwa against the major psychedelics—psilocybin mushrooms, LSD, peyote, DMT, etcetera—explored in the 1960s helped inspire new generations to seek out different tools and invent new substances. A cadre of outsiders has made this forbidden territory their own—such as the chemist Sasha Shulgin who has created hundreds of new psychedelic compounds, opening a Pandora's Box of possibilities that will never be closed again, and the entheobotanists Jonathan Ott and Christian Rätsch. Among the substances that were discovered to have psychedelic properties is dextromethorphan (DXM), a synthetic morphine analog, popularly used as an ingredient in cough syrup, inducing intense dissociative experiences at high-doses, with visionary reports of contacting alien entities and ancestor Spirits, as well as entering alien dimensions or mindscapes that challenge our conventional categories and fray the edges of our dualistic language.

In many cultures, shamans use mind-altering compounds, extracted from plants, to induce nonordinary states in which they can heal, prophesy, and seek new knowledge for their tribe. Over time, shamans as well as sorcerors discover that certain substances are their particular "allies," while others don't call to them. When Dan Carpenter discovered DXM, he found his ally, and this book is the story of their relationship. Like most relationships, this one has its share of ups and downs. Closed-eye DXM sojourns are, for Carpenter, an opportunity for freewheeling philosophic inquiry as well as self-discovery. Of course, it is up to the individual reader to decide how seriously to take Carpenter's ruminations and his insistence that he visited the realms of the dead as well as the "hivemind" of some self-assembling superconsciousness, of which we are expressions. The book is enjoyable purely as a wild ride through an interior continent of possibility and perhapsness; Carpenter is wise enough to realize that validation or rebuttal of his ideas can come about only through some eventual consensual process. As he notes, in his investigation he has followed McKenna's plea for more cartographers of inner space, willing to take their trips as datum, providing linguistic maps and conceptual scaffoldings for others to consider, and for the brave to follow.

I have never tried DXM, but much of the territory Carpenter describes is familiar to me from my explorations of ayahuasca, LSD, and other visionary tools. On ayahuasca, I have found myself seemingly able to access realms of the dead, as though their spirits were indeed suspended in some kind of intermediate Bardo zone. Like Carpenter I have also received particular teachings through visionary states—I especially enjoyed his encounter with the arrogant and destructive English mindset of his ancestors, followed by a meeting with Native American spirits, who comment upon the evolution in attitude that has taken place since then. Like Carpenter, I have been forced to wonder if our modern world has omitted a vast terrain of psychic reality in its quest for materialist dominance.

During the last century, quantum physicists were forced to recognize a depth of interaction between the physical world and human consciousness that made the notion of an observer obsolete—as the physicist John Archibald Wheeler noted, we live in a participatory universe, with no outside place for objective speculation. Although science has demonstrated this, most of us continue to believe that the old materialist paradigm, with its dualistic split between subject and object, still holds. In *The Self-Aware Universe,* the physicist Amit Goswami makes a compelling argument that the paradoxes of quantum physics—nonlocality, Schrodinger's Cat, Heisenberg's Uncertainty Principle, Action at a Distance, and so on—can only be resolved by postulating that mind, rather than matter, is the foundation of the universe. "I had vainly been seeking a description of consciousness within science; instead, what I and others have to look for is a description of science within consciousness," he wrote. "We must develop a science compatible with consciousness, our primary experience." I propose that *A Psychonaut's Guide to the Invisible Landscape* is an early foray in the "science within consciousness" that lies before us. As our understanding of psychic realities deepens, we will realize that the invisible landscapes within the mind deserve as much attention as the physical universe in which we are embedded. Carpenter's book places him on the cutting-edge of those exploring this new terrain.

DANIEL PINCHBECK, AUTHOR OF *BREAKING OPEN THE HEAD: A PSYCHEDELIC JOURNEY INTO THE HEART OF CONTEMPORARY SHAMANISM*

"What we need now are the diaries of explorers.
We need many diaries of many explorers so we can begin
to get a feeling for the territory."
—TERENCE McKENNA IN *THE ARCHAIC REVIVAL*

Preface

In his book *What Makes You Tick?—The Brain in Plain English,* Thomas B. Czerner, M.D., admits that the search for the seat of consciousness was not recognized as a creditable subject of scientific inquiry until 1990! Why is that?

A quick example from *Phantoms in the Brain* by world renown theoretical anatomist V. S. Ramachandran illustrates how, even a progressive guy like this, with his unmatched powers of observation, quickly makes a judgment on alien abduction—seemingly without much thought. "I find it surprising that despite three decades of research, we are not even sure whether these phenomena (stigmata) are real or bogus. Are they like alien abductions and spoon bending, or are they *genuine* anomalies?" (Italics mine.)

I have an uncle who is a respected physicist, schooled at MIT and a professor at Berkeley. Assuming he would drop his professional demeanor while far from his colleagues on a visit to my parents' house in Pennsylvania, I pressed him with a few questions when I got him alone.

"Surely Uncle Fred, you must have *some* personal thoughts as to why light behaves both as a wave and a particle in the double-slit experiment. Could it be that consciousness itself is somehow affecting the outcome?" I dared.

This was the moment. I thought: *He's gonna shift his eyes right to left, lean in and whisper . . .* "It's all due to parallel universes bleeding through the continuum and interfering with the results of the measurements at the quantum level of. . . . " Instead all he would give his humble nephew was something like: "Science can't be bothered by anything to do with philosophy. Nobody really understands quantum theory. We can only use it like a tool. We can never ask why we are able to use it."

(Ph.D. *does* stand for "doctor of philosophy," right?)

It took me a long time to finally grasp where he was coming from—a true scientist has to take a stand for the measurable, and live and breath it. For people like my uncle, there is never a time for personal musings on unprovable phenomenon. While I can respect and understand the absolute importance of that approach, it is not enough for me.

Even as a child I felt unsatisfied by people's assertion that dreams were not important. Being told, "It's only a dream kid . . . go back to bed," was an early red flag for me that people were willing to disallow mystery. As a teenager I began keeping a dream-log (which I have continued, off and on, for about twenty-five years). I also read the entire Bible in those years—quite on my own. I can remember asking a pastor to explain Isaiah 45:7, "I form the light and create darkness, I bring prosperity and create disaster; I the Lord, do all these things." He could only mumble something about "God's ultimate purpose." (It took me years to shake off my self-induced fear of hellfire and damnation, and I wonder how far along I would be "spiritually" if I had never bothered with my investigation of Christianity.)

When I was about eighteen I took my first hit of LSD. I remember returning home sometime after the peak of the trip, and having a deep realization that my entire experience growing up was founded on nothing! I suddenly understood that we all spoke in an almost phony way to each other, to maintain a cordial front—and the complete absence of talk about anything remotely unpleasant was laid bare. I went to my room, and lying on my bed in the dark I realized that the whole world was like this—through and through—from homeless panhandlers to world leaders.

That night was the beginning of the slow erosion of my interest in practicing established religion.

Years later I was thumbing through a used book bin at a thrift store when I found Robert Monroe's *Journeys Out of the Body*. I knew nothing about out-of-body experiences except that people had reported them in near-death states. It seems odd to me now that I came across that book when I did, because I was right in the middle of suddenly having tremendous luck with lucid dreams at the time. Merely considering the possibility that people were really having out-of-body experiences and that their reports were true, I am certain, opened the way for my first one (without any psychedelics) on December 27, 1996.

Through years of studying and cross-referencing my dreams in journals, inducing lucid and out-of-body experiences, and gleaning insight into the very fabric of who or what I am through the use of psychedelics, I have made my own mind my laboratory.

It is easy for people outside the psychedelic community to

roll their eyes at this idea, since there is no way to authenticate something as intangible and fleeting as an out-of-body experience or visions experienced in psychedelic states. There are phony people in every area of endeavor (the Pet Psychic comes to mind). But this should not dampen the quest of the serious searchers, who at least know for themselves that they are on to something big.

The fact that one's awareness can leave the body completely intact and coherent is incontestable to me—and my testimony will have to do as far as proof for scientific scrutiny. In the end these phenomena, I am sure, will prove to be the path missed by science, as the human mind evolves further and the spiritual path finally, inevitably, intersects that of science.

Until such a day comes along, people interested in this kind of thing must be satisfied with being the lone witness when they have an experience like leaving their body or encountering alien beings in the psychedelic trance.

There are things we can know absolutely—things that require no faith to believe in—and that offer the only real hope anyone is going to find concerning death. Each one of us is uniquely qualified to probe the possibilities of our own awareness, and to draw our own conclusions about what we have been told are impossibilities. When that which is being searched for is that which is searching, I believe we are tapping into the most valid source of insight into life's biggest mysteries we will ever make use of.

Introduction: Setting Out on the High Dose Trip

This is meant to explain how I got to a point where I had minimized dangerous or scary situations, and got the trip/trance almost to a routine. IT IS NOT MEANT AS A GUIDE AND SHOULD NOT BE THOUGHT OF AS FOOL-PROOF! I am always apprehensive about entering this state—there is just no getting used to giving up one's ego.

The high doses were taken over the course of a few hours, never all at once. I found that if I "primed" my system with about 300 to 400 mg and waited about an hour, I could then administer more, perhaps 200 mg every twenty minutes, until I could feel myself climbing faster. I would have the amounts laid out beforehand so I wouldn't get off track with how much I had done as I became enveloped in the dissociative effects.

Waiting for the punch to my ego that was imminent was often unnerving, so I would read a book.

Somewhere along the line the words would become things of curiosity—I would catch myself contemplating the words as phenomenon and know it was time to put a pillow over my forehead and eyes.

At this point I would be at about 800 mg. This amount is a big ride and most peak experiences were probably happening in this range. When I reported amounts of 1500 mg, that would be the total for the night. As I exploded into these realms, I could sense the peak at times (DXM's peek is fairly abrupt). Then I would dose back up with another 200 to 300 mg.

The key to navigation is to wait for the ego to be flattened. After the initial uneasiness of turning one's self over, the anesthetic effect allows what is left—the Anti-Ego—to begin its travels. There is little warning of encounters with the Other the first few times out. After a few trips I could ignore them somehow. (It seems that they had gotten used to me and would ignore me as well.)

In the early stages, green lines of swirling light envelope the Anti-Ego. This can sometimes create illusions, by way of the lines taking on what at first appear to be spatial distances. They can even take on the look of giant machines descending down onto one. But this is not the Taffy-Clouds. They come next. The lines of light give way to the "lava in zero gravity." At first this goes on as a long floating in the clouds, without much else. If nothing happens in awhile, it's time to dose up some more.

Eventually there comes the shiny spots in the distance. Locked onto by the peripheral vision, one moves slowly toward, and then into the opening.

Surprise! It may be an Other. Or a laboratory of technology. If not, look further out . . . another shiny spot. Lock on and move into it. From this deep in-Hive, there needn't be any more explanation.

Before each trip I would take a few B-Complex, a multivitamin and a xanax or valium. These benzos, I understand from the DXM faq (at Erowid.com), may help prevent brain damage (as well as, for me, acting as a crutch—albeit basically a placebo given the tiny amount used . . . a 10 mg valium or 1 mg xanax). The morning after I would take another benzo or two just to ease myself back into the world.

Finishing this book has lifted a burden from me. I can now refer people to these writings instead of having to retell the story every time the subject of death or religion pops up in a conversation! I am glad to be able to bring to people's attention the reality of DXM's ability to transport one to this place—the Hive Mind—and that this Hive can be accessed and repeatedly navigated through with considerable control (given, that is, considering the fact that I am talking about a psychedelic experience).

I will, on occasion, in the future, return to the Hive. But my major explorations are over. What I have not reported I leave for myself to ponder.

I believe the vanguard Over There will be made up of the most unconditioned and immaterially minded people who leave this world—and certainly a great concentration of those people are those who have experienced the psychedelic.

Part I: Psychedelic Passageways

Psychedelics and
the Wilderness
of the Mind

Psychedelic states of mind are difficult to convey. For those who have tried LSD or DMT and the like, rendering the experience through words is always problematic. Adequacy in relating what is occurring during a psychedelic trip may have its fundamental flaw in the way knowledge is perceived in these states. Revelations come in wordless knowledge and using language to explain the experience of a completely new way to perceive knowledge means that metaphors or impressions will have to suffice. People who have not had the experience can never be made to understand it.

Questions like "Who am I?" or "Why am I here?" do not or cannot exist as what we think we understand a question to be, when the psychedelic breaks the familiar link with the syntax we have always used to enforce how we think our consciousness works. Even the concept of a question is a part of the conditioned self and, though it may seem absurd, a question has no place after a point. We enter ways of thinking that are foreign to us—and by that very reason we find it hard to translate when the experience brings us into an intuitive grasp of the essential nature or meaning of something. There is knowledge that exists in the Wilderness which has no language.

Having said that, I would also like to add that mastery over interpretation of this silent knowledge, however harrowing the means, is a worthy goal, and one that I have found to be obtainable to some degree, through repeated closed-eye trip/trances. Navigation became the key to returning to the same "places" where, at times, the visions would be of the same subject matter (my ancestry or lineage was one such doorway that repeatedly opened for me).

There is a way to sense this idea of knowledge without language in our everyday lives. I happen to be an accomplished musician of some twenty-five years. A fellow musician and I have had some long discussions on music as a mood altering phenomenon. "Why?" we asked, can the stroke of one major chord sound pleasant or uplifting, and a single minor chord make us feel somber or sad? What we theorized isn't as important to the subject at hand as is the fact that music (without considering lyrics) absolutely IS a language.

(But why can we be made happy or sad by hearing certain tones in certain contexts? My friend and I concluded that this is because dissonant, inharmonious sounds are reminiscent of howling wolves, and a visceral foreboding is tapped upon hearing these tones, which stirs our survival instincts. Happy melodies might be calming to the psyche because of their similarity to bird or cricket sounds. And birds or crickets chirping around us is always a sign that, for the moment, there are no lurking predators about. Or more plainly, a violin or guitar solo can mimic the sound of crying, which stirs empathy.)

I have heard it argued that the word "drug" should not be used when referring to psychedelics, and I am inclined to agree. Using psychedelics is not going to get a person "high" or "stoned"—these substances are "mind-altering"—and that is an apt description. Calling them "self-altering" would have made what they do even more clear. This stuff goes to work on *who you are.* Calling the duration of the effects a "trip" is an accurate description as well.

The psychedelic experience calls into question everything we think we know about ourselves. Questions we might have about reality going in to the experience are quickly revealed as romanticized/idealized notions about what we think we are searching for and are unceremoniously swept aside.

Once, on an LSD trip, the thought came to me that neuroscience is looking from the outside in. I thought: *These brain scientists will never get at it* (consciousness) *because what they are looking for is what is doing the looking!* One thing psychedelics do is to disassociate the ego from an apparently more indifferent part of the self, and a scientist would no sooner want to feel his or her ego slip out from its familiar stronghold than the next person. Their approach might fill volumes of text, but I am convinced that at the end of the search for the seat of consciousness, there must be a showdown with the naked unconditioned and egoless self. (I will give some examples of what I mean further in.) No Ph.D. can prime a person for that. To have an answer requires a forfeiture of that which is asking. Stranger still, as the answer grows near, the seeker is *becoming* the answer—and is yet still the questioner! Where these paths cross is the gateway to the Wilderness of the Mind.

To understand what is being forfeited, there has to be a grasp of what conditioning is, in regard to the self and the self's lifetime of experiences.

With no real answers to life's big questions, the easy direction for most people is into the Known. What is the Known? I believe it can be confidently surmised that, over thousands of years, beliefs arose around, and were reinforced by survival needs initially. As survival needs gave way to more and more luxury, the original purpose of the lore surrounding survival strategies continued to mutate far beyond the reasons for its origins, into religious and political expressions. Many beliefs have certainly become directionless and pathological. With every human death their origins dim, and they twist and branch out in endless self-validating systems. And while these mutating systems have been part of the success of Homo sapiens, psychedelics reveal them to have no relevance to the underlying being.

These are the systems we have inherited. And this is where the unraveling of conditioning must begin.

I read the book *Meditation: The Art of Ecstasy* by the Eastern mystic Bhagwan Shree Rajneesh, and although I soon abandoned meditation (due to my complete inability to bestill myself) I came away with a general understanding of what conditioning is—that I am an infinitely conditioned being, and most of what I think "I" am is actually layer upon layer of conditioned beliefs. My eyes were opened by that book and I regard it as one of the most important books I have ever read. To read about conditioning and realize the depth of its influence on what drives one's motives is, however, a baby step next to the psychedelic experience.

We are born with our awareness tethered to a body, riding on a giant ball of rock hurling through space, and the only thing we can be sure of is that we all must die. And no one knows how or why this is so, yet everyone is caught up in self-importance and how other people perceive them or is busy pointing out flaws in others' demeanors or conduct or ways and looks. How is this possible? How can the whole world of people seemingly go about as if they are immortal?

Fear . . . of who they really are and where they are going, and what it all means.

Most people are afraid to tell you what they're thinking at any one moment, never mind the complete stripping of all that conditioning they have always believed to be a part of themselves. Only thoughts of death might cause more dread in the heart of the self-aware ape in us all, than having to face the fact that we don't know WHAT we are.

Humans are a confused and sad bunch, though hardly anyone is willing to concede this. As we struggle to emerge from millions of years of primal survival hardwiring, we find ourselves in an odd place. We are juggling to keep the field of moral ideals—which we have convinced ourselves is omnipotent—while living with our gene-driven impulses to do whatever will put us and our families in a better position for survival/luxury than the next group of people. And we can never think our way out of our own thinking! We like to believe we have it together—that we have become worthy of self-respect. When things go wrong we all look around for the "evil" that has breached the defenses and cast its shadow on the Light of the World.

To break down the age-old walls of conditioning by use of psychedelics is to reveal ourselves to the Unknown. To do it successfully we must be able to recognize our fear as the survival fail-safe that it is, and be able to suspend that fear—and somehow reassure the ego that its seat will be returned to it after a few hours. (Not always an easy task!)

So what are the advantages in doing psychedelics? I will expound on psychedelics as a spiritual path later, but a couple of quick examples are: the rooting out of materialism, and an understanding of motivation in one's self and others.

But psychedelics will always be a hard sell it seems. What they are showing us (that we don't really know ourselves) *is as real and unsettling to most people as death.* If that statement seems extreme, we need only to ponder the towering mystery surrounding the origin of awareness, to realize that death is an inescapable part of that mystery. We all take birth for granted, feeling secure that, for now we have at least found ourselves here, alive, and so turn our fear toward the possibility that our awareness might somehow be unmade at death. (Considering that we don't remember being "around" before we were born, we might even think of birth as the greater mystery.) So, though perhaps conveyed in some unrealized reservation of mind, psychedelics remind us of death, because the temporary unmaking of the self, for all it can reveal, is what they do. This makes them a thing to fear and that fear extends itself everywhere inside the Known, to include wanting to forbid others from venturing into the experience.

There has been plenty written on psychedelics and politics, and I am much more interested in what psychedelics can show us. So let us move on, to discourse on the experiences themselves.

I am going to tell of some discoveries I have made—some I have not yet found in any trip reports, while others seem to be corroborated in them. (One such corroboration I have experienced several times was something like the "Overmind" Terence McKenna described in *The Archaic Revival*—a kind of giant soul comprised of all of humanity's awareness.) I have done my best to not make these writings just a gathering of trip reports, but instead I am hopeful, more like the journal of a naturalist landed on a new planet. I have used quotes from my journal and tape recordings made during the trips, but, as well, I interject extensively along the way on what I came to believe these events were showing me. (I must say quickly that I have found trip reports on places like Erowid.com to be immensely useful and interesting. It is a fortunate thing to have these available for cross-referencing and crisis prevention—not to mention insight into the self with others doing the hard part!)

Dissociates

Dextromethorphan HBr or DXM is a profound mind-altering dissociative and psychedelic. I have written strictly on my experiences with this stuff due to its anesthetic effects, that allow for closed-eye trip/trances much easier than the more speedy psychedelics. And there is absolutely nothing in the world of psychedelics comparable to closed-eye trips. (I will cover what "dissociative" implies and why that word fits, later.) After much research on places like Erowid.com, I began experimenting with low doses of DXM powder (about 350 mg).

I had had enough mind-bending rides on LSD to prepare myself for what promised to be a strange experience. Of course when doing this sort of thing, expectations are never enough. But after two low dose experiments I felt ready to go ahead into the so-called fourth plateau. (Users report that there seems to be four levels, or plateaus, depending on the dose, each with effects not inherent in the others.)

DXM is often played off as a "kiddie" psychedelic because obviously bored and broke teens do use it, and then post on drug information Web sites, "dude, I was sooo ripped, like worse than drunk. . . ." The most common and undignified method of getting DXM to the brain—drinking cough syrup— has certainly kept it relegated to the status of a poor man's drug in the minds of many cellar-shamans. (Please do not go out and drink any old cough syrup. Some have ingredients that will kill you if you chug too much. I must mention too that anything over 700 mg is a very big ride—things start to get quite freaky. The potential for a full blown freak-out on high doses of DXM is high for anyone who has never done a psychedelic, or even the occasional LSD or psilocybin user uninitiated into the dissociative family. I am saying: low doses at first! It is possible to forget that you've taken anything on high doses. I will tell of some of my close calls later.)

Dissociative anesthetics, as they are called, include: ketamine (known as Special K or simply K), nitrous oxide (laughing gas), phencyclindine or PCP (know as Angel Dust), and finally DXM, which, as I said, I will cover in detail due to my in-depth investigations into the strange and sometimes dark worlds it has shown me. What I have accomplished in the ten or so times I did over 1000 mg can be verified, I am certain, if one uses the means of navigating in a closed-eye trip/trance that I established over the course of these trips. (Basically, it's using a sort of third eye and staring at a point ahead, which draws one to that point.)

One of the more exclusive proclamations I have recorded—that I have witnessed the seat of dreaming—could be investigated in a clinical environment for dream research, like the sessions recorded by Dr. Rick Strassman in his book *DMT: The Spirit Molecule.* (More focus would be on *navigation* in repeated, closed-eye trip/trances.) I do not mean to imply that I have laid to rest the mystery of dreams, but I have been left with insight by my tenacious observation. Without neuroscientists or people conducting dream research looking into psychedelics and means of navigation, the search for answers to the riddle of dreams and consciousness as a phenomenon is crippled—this seems obvious. And so the quest lies open to the great many people like me who are finding out perhaps the most important discoveries right under the nose of neuroscience. The standard search for consciousness within the brain is based on a fundamentally flawed assumption that psychedelics and many writers of metaphysics have revealed. What neuroscience has missed is the single most important line of reasoning . . . that THE BRAIN IS IN THE MIND! (More on this idea later.)

Another exceptional operation I found myself in while navigating in a DXM trance was that of befriending my other selves—establishing a truce with the many "I"s that inhabit the brain. In his book *Phantoms in the Brain* neuroscientist V. S. Ramachandran devotes his entire view of consciousness in terms of the many phantom selves at work unnoticed in everything we do (ever wonder "who" is really doing the walking as you stroll along window shopping?). I only wish someone with the great powers of observation like Ramachandran would use a psychedelic at least once and have the guts to report his or her experience and what it might be showing concerning consciousness. In the future, the first neuroscientist to do so would be doing groundbreaking science and no longer beating around the bush to maintain credibility among his colleagues. To dismiss psychedelics as an investigation tool for probing the mystery of consciousness is as absurd as imprisoning Galileo without first looking through his telescope!

So here I will share my findings. I consider the task only "unscientific" for those people who do not realize that in the end, science MUST follow. Wilderness does not end on the edge of town and it does not end with the brain. Wilderness is everything, from a piece of algae to a computer—to realms of and beyond consciousness. I believe these findings are repeatable in experiments, however subjective, and I find the path into these studies excitingly open for investigation due to science's almost complete avoidance in this area and the psychedelic's indifference to the scholarly credentials of the user. Why do people shun this stuff when we really know next to nothing about reality? Nothing!

Part II: The Experiences

Trip One

Multiple Personalities

Trip One 1/5/03: (900 mg) My first high dose of DXM took me by surprise. I didn't record anything about it because there wasn't much to say except my personality was split up—"me" had become "us"—"I" became "we." I was a little put off by this uncomfortable sense of being scattered and spent the whole trip pinned to the side of my brain somewhere, unable or unwilling to "move." As you will see, with each successive trip, I began to be able to navigate around my brain and other realms by "pulling" in a spot in the distance—some light or cloud-edge—by "staring" at it, drawing it in or moving toward it by never taking my "eyes" off of it.

Trip Two

Of Life in the Taffy-Clouds

My second trip was a 1200 mg ride into a swirling colored-plastic mindscape during which I found myself privy to the very workings of my brain—an insider's view—which left me sad and horrified and exuberant. I had read about the phenomenon of ego-loss in many trip reports and I thought I knew what people were talking about from my dabblings with LSD over the years. I didn't. What happened to my sense of self while on high doses of DXM forced a fundamental deviation in what I had believed I understood "me" to be. I glimpsed the underpinnings of who or what is in charge of the brain.

I cover the experiences in the order that the trips were taken. With each trip I encountered more and more profound things and I became better and better at navigating the realms I would find myself in. The trips were done lying down with eyes closed for most of their duration.

Notes 2/16/03: The DXM trip doesn't feel like astral realms. I tried to project and found myself hopelessly in my head. I am convinced that the machinelike workings I was witnessing were inside my brain. As the doses kick in (about 200 mg every twenty minutes) "thick" taffylike, vaporous light churns and spills like lava in 0 gravity. . . .

At first I wondered if these "thick lights" or "mind taffy" (which is often reported) was a sort of *thought potential*—thoughts in waiting, that I was witnessing from my vantage point, feeling completely disconnected from these things, yet knowing they were me! Later, as the effects wore off, I could still see them faintly, (with eyes closed) and I could see that they were made up of thousands (millions?) of individual strands of light, like a fiber-optic cable. I thought that I must be seeing the retina at work, or "I" was somewhere in the brain where awareness processes sight.

Notes: I make a mental note: Everywhere I look I am seeing with peripheral vision. I can see perfectly, every detail, but I can't stare directly at anything—with "what" am I seeing?

In my dream logs I have recorded my "scientific" approach in lucid dreams, where, instead of moving into the landscape searching for adventure, I would check to see if surfaces like a tree or wall were "hard" to the touch (they always were). Or, to see if I am "making-up" the scene, I would inspect things like paint flecks on a window sill, or tiny pebbles and grains of dirt on a road. (The paint flecks and tiny grains were there, perceived absolutely as if I were using my physical eyes.) In doing this close observation, it never occurred to me to check if I was able to look directly at a pebble say, because I could . . . stare straight at it as if I were looking at it or handling it in the "real" world. After discovering that everything I was seeing was peripheral in the DXM realm, I paid special attention the next time I had a lucid dream—and yes, I was perfectly able to look directly at any detail. The conclusion: the mechanism with which I was "seeing" on DXM is not the same one as is utilized during lucid dreaming.

Notes: Beyond the taffy-clouds I settled into the trip and I encountered the Golden Wall, something I've read about more than once in trip reports. It is a huge barrier of shimmering yellow light. I can bring the Wall into range by "staring" at one spot on its surface. As I come right up against it I can see minute detail—it is not smooth but bumpy and pitted and does not change. When I stop against the side of it my attention gives way and I'm back in my bed, where I close my eyes again. . . .

I hadn't at this point developed a solid idea as to what this wall might be. I though it might be a visual manifestation of the Memory Barrier that causes the memory of dreams or insight gleaned during the psychedelic experience to be squelched even as one tries to assimilate them into everyday reality. This might be part of the story with the Wall, but later I found a further connection between it and the way memory is stored in the brain.

> Notes: In the caverns of taffy; I have begun to notice
> tiny lights and shapes that seem to be knowing,
> aware molecule-like things. They are perfectly
> defined, moving in orbits and performing maneu-
> vers and tasks.

In and beyond the Taffy-Clouds these "molecules" abound and I would later "see" them during every trip. Right away it is apparent that these things are *doing* . . . performing tasks in tight choreographic maneuvers—going about their *duties* in a very animated and no-nonsense way. They are brightly colored, sometimes striped blue and black, or yellow and red—every color is represented in some part of their dance. They come circular or barrel shaped, amid tendrils of green plasma, and at times whole clouds of tiny light spots will cluster and move together like a school of fish, glowing like neon orbs. I am reminded of what electrons might look like in a computer program if one could observe them in action. From my first encounter with these things, I knew without any reservations that I was "seeing" life. Were these things me? A part of my brain, or some Other?

> Notes: At one point I was interacting with an invis-
> ible "person." I was befriended by someone who
> was merrily explaining about these green electric
> tornado-like vortices that were whirling in the

distance. "If you enter one of these your ego will be put back together," the male voice explained. Later as I came out of some forgotten state of the trance (after an apparently lengthy lecture I had been receiving) the voice trailed away saying, "You have to get off here now."

This was my first encounter with some Other being. Later I would get much closer to the life to be found in these realms. The Ego Vortex, too, I would interact with and discover amazing things about how my emotions work; an eerie detached view of "me"—the old me, the one who had always regarded emotions as a given part of who I am.

Trip Three

The Diminished Importance of Emotion

Notes 3/13/03: (1200 mg) Deep within the taffy chambers. My companion from before seems to be back. He shows me a churning flesh colored wheel. I can make out nodules on it like fleshy pimples. All at once I realize that this "wheel" is me—or more accurately my emotional center! This is the Regulator—the place where emotions are sorted. This was revealed when I "witnessed" my emotions in a state of flux, and being expressed randomly to a completely indifferent "me" as a bizarre rollicking wheel of voices-attached-to-emotion (I could actually "see" this wheel by some means). The emotions were actuated from the blending of a few basic "feelings" (the way four areas on the tongue work to create endless flavors in the brain)—but "I" couldn't feel any emotion at all. As the emotions spiraled out they were accompanied by voices that were coming from an area of the brain where every voice I'd ever heard is stored . . . so that an embarrassing parade of voices, from Porky Pig to Ronald Reagan, poured forth in a frightening attempt at expression. (This sense of embarrassment, too, the "I" through which the experience was most subjective couldn't feel. This "I" is the Anti-Ego.) This Regulator of Emotion had always been "me" but now it was simply "mine." It had gotten loose—now on its own, crying and laughing, goofy and serious—driverless—having lost its counteridentity, with which it needs to maintain a mutual agreement, in order to decide which emotion should be tapped to fit the circumstance in the everyday life of the self. . . . What might this mean to criminologists studying serial killers? Or the study of schizophrenia?

These notes speak for themselves here, but the way I felt after finding out that my emotions were but a tool, built-in to "me," is beyond words. I thought: *Doesn't anyone in science know about this?* This experience was so real and so keenly felt, yet so threatening to my belief system—and everyone's for that matter—that I was confused as to what I should do with this knowledge. Who could I tell? A shrink? Not likely! My friends already thought I was delusional from trying to explain about my out-of-body experiences. So I kept it to myself and went hunting for books on the brain. (I did try to raise the idea on a few Web sites devoted to psychedelics, but even there the idea of emotions being "not real" was quickly brushed off.) But for me, this was only the beginning of more unsettling discoveries. . . . They were fascinating too though, and I resigned myself to look deeper into it all, like a reporter, whatever lay out there. I would eventually interact with the Ego Vortices—those green spirals of light my "tour guide" had spoke of.

Liquid Technology

Notes (Trip Three): I was attempting to draw into range another spot in my peripheral field. As the area I locked onto came closer I sensed that it was a being this time. I understood instantly that it was aware of me. It had the appearance of converging lines, a "face" like a splayed crab or radiating cables, or like the inlay design on a showy gun. It was alive, and yet it was made of "liquid metal"—a kind of organic/metallic blend. I remained connected visually to it as it hovered and moved in (at this point I'm "emotionless" and not feeling one way or the other about danger). It finally made contact and at that instant, it injected itself into me! It probed me very nonchalantly. I ended up frozen, resting pinned somewhere like when I found myself resting against the Golden

Wall. Having nowhere left to go, I found myself put out of the trance and leaned over to outline these notes.

In later trips I encountered many of these Other. At first I called them "liquid robots," more for the apparent indifference to my feelings they exuded than anything mechanical about them—they were alive, organic, yet somehow a technology as well. Later I named them the Crab Faced Other due to the converging line/tentacles that seemed to make up their "face." The oddest part of being injected by the Crab Faced was that I got nothing out of the exchange—no sense of, "Oh, that's fantastic. I understand!" Why then did it do that?

At the time of the encounter, "I" was the stripped-down Anti-Ego. This state of "not me" was, as described by others in trip reports on dissociatives, a third person account of the action. I call this state the Anti-Ego because "I" am there, a thinking someone, still mostly myself but missing something. Or Was I? Emotions again. I was beginning to sense that this state might be more "me" than the other "me" that I was used to being. Whatever qualms the old "me" might have—and there were plenty—I was not going to allow them to interfere in the name of discovery. I thought: *This must be what one becomes after death. This must be the real me, I'm just not used to it yet.*

One thing I was surprised to find in the DXM reports was a lone mention of "furniture" by one guy. As I continued plunging into the Taffy-Clouds, I began to slow down and hover into crevasses or cavelike openings that "felt" reminiscent of a honeycomb though not structurally. I could make out fine detail of what I knew somehow to be living quarters. There were "appliances" and "couches" made out of the living Hive Mind itself. The appliances were the molecule-like, knowing things again, zipping around each other at their tasks. Everything including the Crab Faced Other seemed to be made of some combination of the same plasma/plastic/metal/organic/living material. The whole labyrinth was all one organism. But on a smaller scale it was like an ant colony with individual members.

Breaks in Time

Notes (Trip Three): Sometime around the peak of the trip a terrifying event happened that I handled by the seat of my pants. . . .

I would do these trips over at a friend's house and she would leave me to my visions in a room down the hall from the living room where she would watch TV and keep an ear out for me. (She is a registered nurse and a practitioner of the occult, and although psychedelics are not her thing, she enjoys hearing about my experiences.)

What happened was I started feeling unsettled somehow, but I was too far gone to assess what it might be. I came out of the room, crawling, and said, "I think I could use a bath." My friend didn't question me but went to draw a bath. As I crawled after her my internal clock went off-line. The world kept coming over me as a new world—one I had just entered—a reality I had just arrived in. Each time this happened I had to create a new scenario about who and where I was. I said: "I am Dan

Carpenter! I am an earth man!" Then the world was new again.
I thought: *I've fucked up this time! I live on a planet right?*

"Water's ready!"

"Beth? Oh right! I am Dan Carpenter! I am an earth man!"

As I sloshed in the bathtub, there was a full second between
each of my arrivals into reality. And each time, because I would
move, my new view would be from a foot or so away from my
view the second prior. This was the "strobing" often reported
on DXM (where everything around you is perceived as if a
strobe light had been turned on). But the strobing was now
stretched out into full seconds—a duration too long for me to
maintain a continuity about reality.

I wouldn't let on to my friend exactly what I was going
through, except to say, "I've had some kind of break. You're
there right?"

"Yes, I'm sitting right here."

"Am I a God or something? What's happened?"

"No! You're tripping remember? Breathe deep and slow.
Remember you said to give you this message if you needed
it: 'It's only the drug.' Remember?"

"Oh right. I'm Dan Carpenter. . . ."

This was the first time I had ever really felt like I needed a sitter. I was glad to hear her voice as I struggled for the next twenty
minutes (as she later told me it was) in this discontinuous state.

I was paying a high price for that experience at the time. But
later I would be back, full into it again. And I would find out
more about these "flashovers" as I came to call them—actually
getting used to them, saying casually to my friend when they
hit, "I'm flashing over," which simply meant it was time for
her to guide me once again to the bathtub. (The baths worked
wonders and the intensity of this event eventually waned.)

Trip Four

The Ego Vortex

Notes 4/4/03: (1300 mg) I drifted over a scene that looked like a concert but had the vibe of a postbattle scene as well. . . .

This was somehow attached to the emotional centers (the Ego Vortices from earlier). There was a chord ringing out, like a big sounding barre chord on an electric guitar. It was musical but it didn't change. The chord just hung there droning. As I passed over a field of "people" (or awareness that felt human) I could feel the collective emotion of remorse coming off of them. They, and me, were feeling it together—inspecting remorse—and suffering it together.

Then, one of the most telling events. I came over one of the Ego Vortices, orbiting it (it was circular, or like looking at a tornado from a side view). As I floated around it my emotions were being fed to me, instead of coming from me, so that as I passed over it, "I" (the Anti-Ego) felt disgust or dislike—but only for a second. In the next instant "I" was being attenuated by degrees so that "I" was quickly feeling indifferent to the object. Only for another second, and "I" was feeling glad to be near it . . . I now "liked" it! Emotions were being spread across my psyche with no context, so that I was "feeling" them in a pure form. (This reminds me of the music analogy, in that music can create a longing for which the listener has no context, no reason he or she can put a finger on, so that the emotion's origin is a mystery. And so music becomes a mystery.)

This, after my encounter with the Regulator, had driven the realization home—"I" was independent of "my" emotions. As unwelcome as this idea was to me, I soon came to grips with it. And my navigation skills were quickly increasing—I believe due to my willingness to accept that I may be, ultimately, a being who can use emotion if I wanted, or I could exist without it just as well. Being without emotion was not as bleak as it might at first seem, because I was actually not emotionless either. There was awe and fascination and dread passing through me, but something was gone. Call it animal emotion. I discovered that we humans have many defenses even in our most rational states, tangled up in our feelings. It's the ego—self-validating its existence in a feedback loop. The idea that *any* emotions might be superfluous is argued away by the ego automatically when called into question. (Perhaps you are feeling that now while reading this?)

These notions are not what people want to find out about themselves. However this is my testimony. I didn't make it up. The spiritual path is somewhere, free of pettiness, and that is something foreign to the way we think and react. Anyone with enough guts can verify this. Over and over I was shown things about emotion and each time the theme was—EMOTIONS ARE TEMPORAL.

Meeting Myselves

Notes (Trip Four): (Tape-recorded.) "I'm being taken on a guided tour. Presented with or rather introduced to myself, parts of me. It would be like shaking hands with myself . . . these intricate patterns and wires. I looked just like the Crab Faced, at least in the face. The part of me that I would confront was a group of cables or converging lines. I thought of the common insectoid theme reported on DMT and I could understand why people sensed this. It did have a kind of insect look or feel to it. . . . I feel infantile describing myself because I am off to the side. There's machinery, intent, and I am it, yet aside, wondering how I'm/it's ordered or where the order is and how I can search properly for the mind over brain . . . TV voices again."

This meeting between the selves started out very slowly. I was extremely cautious because this sort of thing is utterly taboo. It's madness—everyone knows if you talk to yourself you're off the deep end! My bravado to act like a reporter whatever I encountered was being seriously challenged.

I was navigating around my brain and feeling like I was perhaps only one-third myself. "I" was the stripped down ghost of the former "me." Out among the neurons was something that wanted to talk, and it didn't want to be frightened either. The stored voices were being tapped. As loony as it might seem to have Bart Simpson do the talking, it was nonetheless a very sober and serious moment.

Gingerly a TV voice broke out. The first couple of words were perhaps Alan Alda: "Is that me?"

"Yes," (one third of me) said.

"Are you afraid?" said Andy Taylor.

"Maybe. I don't wish it though," said "I."

"We don't, too," said Peter Jennings, George Carlin, and SpongeBob Squarepants.

I thought: *Whoa! We?* And so it went for a few moments until "I" drifted to some other area within the Hive.

This fraternizing with myself would pick up now during each subsequent trip. I felt uneasy about it on some level—like one wrong turn and all the "I"s might get tangled up and full blown schizophrenia might ensue.

Notes: I have been injected by a few different beings now. The Crab Faced Other. I don't feel these are me now. Or they are in the sense that the Hive Mind is all one thing. But even so, there must be a kind of suspended belief in that oneness, just as there is in everyday reality. I tried an experiment that got me into trouble. . . . In mid-connection with one of the beings, I pulled out vigorously, ripping away from it and opening my eyes. Not good! I sat up and my mind was, well, severed. Ultimate terror rippled through me. I knew it was useless to give in to it. Luckily some vestige of me was able to say: "Okay, this is bad. Just walk it off." There was turmoil on the other side as well. It seemed the thing I had ripped away from was angry or confused. There was a feeling of racism! Others had come to the aid of the Other and were accusing me of being racist! I was walking around the house at this point with my brain/mind divided still. I can only describe it as being left in parts, and unlike the gentle way I'd drifted apart before—when I was able to be apart by degrees and drift with the feeling—now I was completely disconnected in a seriously uncomfortable way. I pleaded with the "guy" I'd insulted, saying, "Yes, I must have some prejudice in me somewhere! Help me to remove it!" I felt like I was making a deal, and slowly I regained myself.

This was the first indication that the Hive Mind had its problems, just like the human struggles on earth. By this point I had decided that this Hive Mind must be the Overmind described by Terence McKenna in *The Archaic Revival,* a living Super Mind made up of all of humanity—a place of the dead—forging itself into one mind. Evidence for this idea would grow with every trip. It was self-aware, but it didn't have all the answers either. There is politics in the Overmind!

Visions of Strife

Notes (Trip Four): I am convinced now that I am
being shown things. I am able to navigate into the
Hive with increasing ease. But at certain intervals
I am inundated with a scene that is flashed across
my awareness like a documentary film. I was shown
a poor black woman with children living on an
American street. Then I was given a glance back
in time and shown the deep pain of the American
black people—slavery. I saw a montage of chains
and wooden pens where strong adult black men
were housed. I could feel their torment. This wound
is deeper than I could have ever imagined.

This was the beginning of what can only be called Visions. It
was absolutely a purposeful series of pictures—but pictures
I was emotionally connected to. (Though I would be disconnected and in the Anti-Ego state, I was able to share the utter
despondency of the slaves.) Then, something amazing. . . .

Notes: I was taken back to where I pulled away
from the Crab Faced earlier. It seems it was actually a black guy. The "thing" that fused with me
was "human" and he lives in the Hive. There was a
sense of reconciliation over the "racism" incident.
The guy took me into his "apartment" and I could
"feel," not hear, music—and it was funk music!

At this juncture I was trying to gather enough "evidence" that these Crab Faced were not predators like the inorganic beings described by Castaneda in the don Juan books. I had seen this black man's face as a group of cable/tentacles—and it was the Crab Face. The Hive was full of humanity and we looked like insects! But was it all a trick?

Around this time I began to notice that there were other things hovering around me. At first I thought they were the "molecules" from before, but it began to dawn on me that these things were homing in on me—following me! These were not the busy, indifferent "appliances"—these were another species of Other. They had tiny glowing "eyes" on the end of stalks, and bodies like swirled, multicolored plastic/plasma. I named them the Plasma Flowers (they look plantlike—I once described them as "twisted bird cages" during a trip). They would later "come out" every time I entered a high dose trip/ trance. I felt like they were somehow mischievous. At times they would hover in a chamber of the Hive and entice me to follow. "What about my body?" I once asked. They seemed to only "giggle." At one point I "asked" them to come in closer, that I might remember what they looked like to later render them in a painting. They were only too glad to oblige. They swung in "chittering" (soundlessly)—they felt like a group of bullies humoring me. I think the sense of something disturbing about them comes from the way they "feel" on a visceral level—like they are one-minded . . . intelligent but out for themselves. Still, I liked them and found them fascinating and beautiful.

Dream Police

Notes (Trip Four): I started to run into "Agents."

This is a subject I am only going to touch on lightly. There is a hierarchy in the Hive just like on Earth. There are "soldiers" about. The most I will say is that they are on familiar ground over there and have means of rendering the neuronaut overwhelmed at the touch of a "hand." To get out of a situation, I made a promise not to tell certain things about them. It was real enough for me to accommodate their wishes. . . .

A Tour of the Brain

Notes (Trip Four): Being shown some parts of my brain—definite damage.

This was a view on a molecular level. I could see torn and burned-out fleshy cells dangling or floating useless. This was followed by a warning. . . .

Notes: (Speaking into a tape recorder.) I was just injected by something that said, "Learn something different, something new." Freaky man! Some kind of robot thing again. Wow! No two ways about it . . . that was a thing that just came down and like . . . reset my programming. Whew! That's absolutely what happened, unbelievable. They're communicating!

If these things were predatory, would they bother warning me? Warning me of what? The damage I was doing with DXM? That's the only conclusion I can as yet come up with.

Reintegration of the Selves

Notes (Trip Four): I seem to be more together now. The sense of being split up has reversed. Many instances of trade/agreement/lessons between the Multi-Selves. The other "I"s anticipate my question before I ask it, because they are privy to the thought as it arises in the consciousness—because they are me! It goes: "Yes, we are here, we are you!" Then "I" say, "Are you there? Is that me?"

Initially, my personality was revealed to be not an "I" but an orchestra of "I"s working in unison to create a sense of one "I." However, either by way of the Multi-Selves relaxing together, or the brain/orchestra regrouping in spite of the chemical, I found myself gradually becoming a single "I" again while in the high dose trance (although still as the Anti-Ego). What happened next is the crux of my theory on dreams and it ties in with the Multi-Selves. . . .

The Dream Chamber
and Some Conclusions

Notes (Trip Four): (Into a tape recorder.) I'm flying over a scene that looks like an elaborate model

> train set. Amazing. . . . What it is is a dream landscape.
> It's a three-dimensional scene of every dream I've
> ever had. I can at this point remember/see every
> dream I've ever had. Now I'm drifting down into it.
> . . . It's like a costume warehouse. Like the inside
> cover of The Allman Brothers' *Eat A Peach* album.
> People, animals, archetypes, childhood monsters
> . . . they're all here! And this is not a memory, but a
> place! Everything still happening—alive—a living
> hologram. Maybe Freud wasn't so wrong.

It seems I was looking at a sentient world of thought—my thoughts!—being the dreams "thought up" by me over a lifetime. I must emphasize: everything in this place was ALIVE still . . . moving, happening.

The idea that the brain is a sort of antenna that receives signals from the mind outside time/space has been raised by many mystics. Amit Goswami, Ph.D., tackles this idea in his book *The Self-Aware Universe.* Of course my approach is direct experience and far from Goswami's grasp of physics in the telling. But direct experience has a gravity all its own for me, and I must report, my experience seems to confirm this notion—*the brain is in the mind.*

I had been musing on and off for some time with the idea that everything—the entire universe—might have been "thought" into existence . . . that it is somehow the Great Thought of some unknowable It. And that we are this thinking It, as well as the thought itself—though in some diminished form here on earth, made so by Our/Its own reason. Although unknown to me during my days of taking DXM, there were philosophers musing along these lines of thinking hundreds of years ago.

Irish philosopher George Berkeley (1685–1753) had an angle called immaterialism. In his 1710 work, *A Treatise concerning the Principals of Human Knowledge,* he wrote: "the observing mind of God makes possible the continued apparent existence of material objects." Berkeley is saying that mindless material substances exist only in our perception of them and that there is no paradox between the mind and the body because the body is the perception of the mind. This is along the lines of Goswami's Self-Aware Universe—the brain is in the mind. Of course there can be endless debates on immaterialism. (What about the obvious sense of pain we experience in the body?)

I'm not going to get too involved with this except to say my hunch is that It is all Wilderness. That is, There and Here are not mutually exclusive. We can, through the psychedelic trance, see into There from Here (this is a fact any serious neuronaut wouldn't argue . . . would have no need to debate). Being able to interface with There from Here is proof enough when one thinks about it, to make obvious that it is all One somehow. Connected. There and Here are boundaries in the same Wilderness.

Modern day philosopher Henry Alphern said of Berkeley in his work, *An Outline History of Philosophy:* "No one can reach beyond his own impression, perceptions and thoughts. [Berkeley] reasons in a circle . . . he desires to conform to a conclusion reached by him in advance." But alas, Alphern's words sound like someone who has never tripped and Berkeley seems to have thought his way near to what quantum physics is saying about reality. (In the double-slit experiment with light, it seems that the observer is tied up in the experiment, so that the behavior of the light, whether it appears to be acting as a wave or a particle, depends on whether it is being observed. Its behavior thwarts any attempt to pin it down as wave or particle, because the experiment is incomplete without the observer. A tree falling in the forest might not only not make a sound, it might not even be there until an observer collapses the potential wave-function—the tree as possibility—into existence by observation. Though I don't pretend to understand anything about these paradoxes, I do understand quantum physicists don't either! A great book for the layperson interested in these odd findings is *Where Does the Weirdness Go?* by David Lindley.)

With the discovery of the Multi-Selves and then the Dream Chamber, I was suddenly struck with a connection between the two that felt reasonable—so much so that I found it hard to believe I had never read about anything quite like what I was beginning to formulate in my mind before.

It has always seemed to me that one of the most important clues to the mystery of dreaming was the phenomenon I call Dream Steering. Often when we dream, an object of one's fancy or lust continues to evade the dreamer. Problems arise in the dream to create hurdles and dead ends (the phone won't dial, the car won't start, roads "conspire" to take the dreamer in the wrong direction). Money, or a person or a place we desire, is caught up in a play that seems to want to run its own course.

What I think is happening is that the longings are stemming from the self experiencing the dream in the first person, the Pure Ego—the "I" At Large—which has shed the tethers of conditioning. Desires flow unchecked through the now childlike "I" who has been left unattended by the more virtuous "I"s (that are perhaps regrouping and organizing beliefs and memories while the body sleeps). But the other phantom "I"s are still keeping tabs on the first person "I," so that a plot twist is injected here and there when these more morally and consciously conditioned other selves see that things are going too far for their liking. Or the plot might be guided and kept from becoming more involved than is necessary, because the Pure Ego is being held in the dreamscape simply to give it something to do during sleep and nothing more. The plot twists caused by the other "I"s are also injected into the dream through the other characters in the dreamscape. These too are the self. It may be that none of the "I"s are aware of the others as self.

Perhaps an alliance between the selves, where useless conditioning is agreed upon by all parties to be shed, is the path to ultimate unity for the orchestrated One (self). From my dealings in this area I can only say that, although the Multi-Selves are part of the One, there exist fail-safes for the prevention of chaos that opt for suspicion over the unknown. Each "I" has been comfortable clinging to its routine of ignorance since the brain/antenna came on the scene, and relinquishing that sense of security is not what any of the "I"s are immediately willing to do. The sense that madness waits is too strong.

The fact that I began to feel together again in subsequent high dose trances hinted at some progress in this area, and surely this is how the approach must be accomplished, by slow introductions all around. (To say to the Selves, "Okay! On three we all drop our security blankets. Ready?" could mean that if there is one hold-out, irreversible panic will ensue.) So, there is politics in the Self!

I am left to conclude that humans are an extension of the

same It/Them from the Hive (which, as I will later show, must be the Dead). We are drops of "living water" from the human pool of awareness in the Hive Mind, that is itself a scaled up version of a single mind. Perhaps the Hive itself is yet again an extension of some Unknowable Great Thought and may be on the verge of joining thoughts with other planets that have burst on the cosmic scene by way of self-realization.

The attempt to describe this hierarchy of awareness, in the end, must fall short of what It really is. All of It is just It. One. There is a line I picked up somewhere of a Buddhist teacher and student: "The voices of torrents are from one great tongue. The lions of the hills are the pure body of Buddha. Isn't that right teacher?"

"It is," said the teacher, "But it is a pity to say so."

It can be reasonably argued that everything I was seeing was in fact only in my brain, and I believe that much of it was. (Here we have to suspend the immaterialist view for the sake of conversation.) If we think about the brain and every fantasy or bizarre image we have ever placed by way of our imagination, into our mind's eye, we generally don't consider the machinery that makes it all possible or the fact that every one of those images still exists, stored somewhere in the memory.

What would the mechanisms for imagination look like?

The inside workings of the brain, seen as I have explained with a kind of third-eye view, gives the impression of a zany, kooky realm that one might at first not take very seriously, believing that it's all somehow the unreal twisting of consciousness due to the psychedelic. But I came to realize that everything in this madhouse was real—it was the brain—waggish, carnivalesque, downright weird, and not at all the lofty machine of perfect wiring, neatly connected like the computer that I had always imagined it to be. (Even in my sanest moments, I am in potentia.)

In his excellent book *Breaking Open the Head,* Daniel Pinchbeck told of seeing his thoughts arise and then evaporate as particles of light while in the ayahuasca trance (ayahuasca is the DMT laden jungle juice of South America). He had seen the neurochemical process of his own thinking and he concluded that thoughts, for the most part, just happen without our initiating them.

I had seen basically the same thing, but I had been hanging around much longer watching this stuff with each new trip. I saw endless bits of floating, living particles, buglike with neon eye/feelers on the ends of stalks. There were multicolored tubes, orbs, and plantlike plastic/plasma formations, the voices of cartoons and the evening news ringing through memory chambers, and messengers like sophisticated leeches running along "wires" and streams of "cables" made of light, all strangely self-aware, looking back at "me." All the crazy comings-and-goings were self-regulated by the parts themselves, like a host of hardened ER doctors in action after a bus crash. The psychedelic had held a door open into one "me," allowing another "me" to see in . . . and "I" was a squirming electric flesh-chemical ant colony.

This is what the showdown with the self is. This raving oddity has to be studied with an absolutely "sober" approach—faced head-on while suspending the urge to recoil at the weirdness of it all being the self. And this stance has to be taken while the ego has been stripped away! Add to this the stigma of using psychedelics and the affect on people's conception of a neuroscientist doing so, and the hurdle for science is clear.

All of my ideals about what the mind might be like I consigned to the trash heap after actually SEEING it from the inside. This is where the layperson, the neuronaut, gets the real news. One look into the multitudes of miniature, living, AWARE parts—this madhouse that is the underpinnings of the rationale we hold so dear—and the gulf between what we are and where science is poking around is laid bare.

Here I found a clue to the stripped down Anti-Ego. To witness these tiny knowing bits of me, by deduction, the "I" in the Anti-Ego state doing the watching, must be incomplete. So the stripped down me feels stripped down because it is existing as a partial self. (This state had become not so strange and I believe, as I have said, that it must be the "real" me—the me that crosses into death. The rest of "me"—these parts at the ready to initiate the knee-jerk survival emotion, or simply tell the heart to beat again, or feed the worrier "me" reasons for concern over food and money—this is what is unmade at death.)

Still, evidence for the existence of Other life, not of the brain or the human feeling Hive, is undeniable when you encounter it first hand. (Quantum Theory tells us that ultimately everything is a cloud of atoms. That everything is mostly space between nuclei in atoms, and the illusion of things that are hard to the touch, arises because of electromagnetic forces. But this knowledge will not help to soothe the nerve endings in your toe when you kick a rock. So it is when we encounter Other life. If the Other is part of the self-aware universe, it must arise from the same source, and be a part of the same emergence of expression. And so too must be a relative of human awareness somewhere down the line. But like the stubbed toe, our sense of separateness forces us to cling to the collective fail-safes in place within the orchestrated everyday self. Anti-Ego state, diminished emotion, stripped down self or not, these Other feel utterly alien!)

The visions are another point of "proof" for me that not everything experienced in the DXM trance originated from chemicals and electricity in the brain. From the Mind outside of the brain comes streaming through lessons, warnings, glimpses of the unimagined—all put together like a documentary. You get the vibe you're not the director—that your will is in abeyance.

Trip Five

Seeking Visions

I began to notice that when a shiny area would appear on the wall of the Hive, something important was about to be revealed. My heart would beat faster as I kept my eye on the spot (which, I have explained, is how I was able to move around, controlling my direction). I would arrive at the shiny spot and move into the cavelike opening where instantly something astounding would happen. The visions would roll and I was no longer navigating—something would take charge and I would be sucked into the "movie."

The Ancestors

Notes 4/24/03: (1400 mg) There are people in tunnels. There is a lunar landscape of living thought (?) and there are men digging tunnels just below the surface. They can see out through small openings in the thought/rock. I am made aware that they are Irish and English men of old. They are working as a team because there is no room to get by one another in the tunnel. The lead man digs and gains knowledge/dirt and shovels it back along the line of men behind, each one passing it in his turn. They absolutely must trust each other and work as one. They work tirelessly and chant with a sense that one day they will dig far enough (to freedom?). I can feel/hear their old accents. Then I'm facing some man of old (England?). He stresses the importance of ancestry, blood lines, lineage. . . .

This man was, as with other human encounters, both seen and felt. He was a knight or some equivalent. Suddenly as he spoke he pointed down a row of nobles. The hair on my neck stood as I realized what he was saying—these men were my grandfathers! I found myself saying, "Twenty-three-year-old Sir George Harrod" (or) "Hadley"—I still do not know why I said it. Was George me in a past life? I had the feeling these tunneling men of old were trying to come to terms with their deep belief systems, working through change bit by bit, curious and skeptical, inspecting every last grain of dirt/knowledge as if it may reveal a trick. They must have thought themselves in hell, but there was a glimmer of slow abatement concerning their beliefs. It is only now, as I write this, that I realize that these men must have been keeping just "underground," with only small openings into the surrounding "land" on purpose—for safety, least they venture out and be caught by the Devil! Their conditioning had been so thorough in life that the poor buggers have been digging for centuries!

However superstitious they may have been, the emphases on the importance of one's ancestors would soon become obvious to me. This I came to find out when, on the highest doses yet, I experienced two near-death situations—and ancestors were the key to getting my bearings at the threshold.

Near-Death Experiences

Notes (Trip Five): (Talking into the tape recorder at trip's peak.) Earthquake? No, the room is shrinking. My idea of what I thought was real is no more. I've just experienced being on a ventilator. At first I was sure it was me—that I had been in a terrible accident. I thought, "All right then. So I'm dead." But then I was next to a guy on a ventilator. He was in a motorcycle accident. He was saying, "Turn off the fucking machine!" To me? He wanted me to tell the doctors or his family. . . . Then it's me again. I've been in a car wreck. I thought seeing the guy on the ventilator was just me passing by a person lingering on the edge of death. I thought, "Poor dude, he'll be along soon enough. But I'm really dead. Now what?" I was swept along. My relatives came out saying, "See? This is all it was! Come with us!" There was a great sense of homecoming.

This was the classic near-death experience. Among the relatives seemed to be my grandmother on my father's side for one. There was even a tunnel, or a slide I had gone through or down. But I saw it more as a curve, I was sliding, being catapulted to my left (?). My relatives were ahead in the distance, aware of me. I never reached them.

In a subsequent trip, it happened again. I found myself accelerating and I instinctively knew: *I've died! This is it . . . wow!* I was made to understand (by what?) that I had run my car off the road. I could feel my leg was broken. Again I took it in stride: "So I'm dead. Now what?" It was the curve/tunnel and the waiting ancestors again. But this time I wanted to know: "When did this happen?"

I was told: "Three months before your thirtieth birthday." But I was forty when I had this experience! Of course it could mean that I got some information wrong. Or . . . did I in fact die at age twenty-nine? And is this life I am living now a respite, an offshoot of that old life? A second chance? Maybe my life began when I "came down" from the trip and was made to believe that I had always been Dan Carpenter!

Outposts of Reality

Notes (Trip Five): There was a sense of constriction in everyday reality. I was swept along and was immersed in the absurdity of my life being something I believed in. It was as if a layer had been peeled back. Something "winked" at me as if to say, "Shhhhh! You see now?" My friend who lived down the road who trip-sat me all the time, the people at Daniel Pinchbeck's Web site, the fact that I'd stumbled on DXM when I did . . . the old man in the

> street I'd given five bucks to, the fact that my
>
> boss had given me three days off, which I'd used
>
> for tripping, was all somehow a program. Every-
>
> thing was visionary . . . both everyday and altered
>
> reality. There is no free will—only the sense that
>
> there is.

I have yet to shake this sense of ALL-AS-PROGRAM. My life seems to be taking on a dreamlike quality. I sense the orchestration of the Multi-Selves on a grander scale . . . the tweaking of the Plot. I am right where I should be. All is déjà-vu-but-new.

There was a "person" looking over a corner of the Veil (which was the corner of the bedroom) like the old "Kilroy was here" drawings, saying: "I'm putting this back into place now! We will insert you here—but as you have seen, we could have put you anywhere and you would be none the wiser!" And as the Veil went up I was again laying in bed, back in my old world. During the time when the Veil was down there was much more revealed that I have lost. . . . I do remember being shown the silliness of my attempt to write a book on this stuff. Silly not because of anything to do with the futility of the endeavor. I sensed more that some "thing" had chuckled like a parent whose kid has built a model rocket proclaiming, "I'm gonna be an astronaut!"

The Buddhist Guides

> Notes (Trip Five): I've been to a kind of Buddhist
>
> gathering. . . .

In trip four, under "A Tour of the Brain" I mentioned how some *thing* " . . . just came down and reset my programming." It happened again, but this time I could sense that it was a man from the Orient! He kind of "tiptoed" across my field of vision and, arriving at an orb or oval piece of technology, he "reset" it—and by "it" I mean some part of me! Sometime after, I found myself drifting over a scene of unmistakable Buddhist monks. I could smell incense. There was a high seat of honor and I understood it was for me. The monks were saying, "He has made it! This is Dan's Day! Place him on the seat!" Where-upon I found myself on this High Seat covered in velvet(?) and framed with silver(?). I felt honored but awkward. As the fan-fare went on, suddenly something went wrong—like the chair broke. I felt odd though not shameful because I was trying to stay neutral about it all—seeing where this would all lead. Then one young man approached smiling and I understood the bro-ken chair had been a cosmic joke of some kind, like a hazing. The young man said: "This is the first enlightenment!" We both began to laugh hardily. But I was laughing using his voice. He was laughing through me, or our laughter had become One Laughing—so that my physical body uttered the high-pitched giggles that were his!

Notes: After the laughing I was adrift again and I saw the unmistakable shiny spot on the Hive wall.

I popped through the opening and I was over a deep dark valley. Rising up from the depths were "silver" candlestick-like objects with dishes at the top. On the dishes were lavender-colored cakes cut into rough squares. There was a man/guide who "told" me, "These are pure love, piled up through the ages. See how they bleed?" And they did. Blood-red spots began to form on the sides of the cakes. I had the feeling that they were hallowed. They were a testament to anguish. I understood that they would never be moved or be used for anything. They were too pure, too concentrated. They were the result of human misery, mostly over lost loved ones, and they needn't be so pure, piled so high. It was the belief in the unmaking of the soul, death the victor, permanent separation, forever, that had wrought these love cakes—anguish had rendered them museum pieces.

Reading and Remembering

For whatever reason I decided to read a book. It was Carlos Castaneda's *The Active Side of Infinity*. Although briefly I was able to follow the text and even hear don Juan's voice, I soon discovered some strange things about the brain as processor. First, I noticed that I was "saying" the words loudly in some chamber of my head. If this process was as noticeable in everyday reality as it was at 1400 mg DXM, it would be impossible to ever relax with a book—the internal voice was simply too "loud."

Then, as my ego touched down briefly, I understood what I was doing . . . reading a book. Nothing so odd about that. But the ego would lose contact with the reader and the reason for reading wasn't so clear. *What are words anyway?* I thought. With the ego suspended I could sense how the brain took in the shapes of the words and didn't really bother with the letters. That is, the whole word was processed like a single shape. One part of the brain saw the negative space around the word, while another shot information back to the place of stored memory. As the Anti-Ego I was blatantly aware that "I" was at times indifferent to what was being said in the text and this is what allowed me to notice the processes as they were taking place.

Then I closed my eyes. I saw the Golden Wall forming, and on it, and into it were flowing the text from the pages of the book! I could see line after line of text pouring onto the Wall like electrosyrup, staining like neat graffiti. As the text filed away, the Wall was hardening into the unmovable, pitted, shimmering thing I had rested myself against before. *This is memory!* I thought. Later it occurred to me that the plain, unstained Walls that I had encountered in earlier trips must be "blank" memory screens, which hovered in place while I viewed them from the third eye, until they "gave up" trying to catch a memory and so "froze" with nothing on them.

This notion might be a stretch I admit, but watching the text from the page of a book form itself into a "screen" and then solidify and drift into the blackness of my mind leaves me with no other conclusion.

The Dead in the Hive

Notes (Trip Five): I drifted past some people freshly deceased. . . .

The Hive, I had realized by now, is a place still growing, sorting itself, trying to establish itself into something of order. There are "back alleys" and "low-rent districts" as well as new unlived-in "Many Mansions." In certain places I encountered people who were, for lack of words, trapped. One in particular was a man of about thirty-five, a blue-collar kind of guy, who was perplexed and talking to himself. He was aware that he was dead and not very alarmed. He was saying: "Where's my place? What do I get now?" He was in a blue crusty place, stuck near the ceiling of something like sheets of frozen blue sugar crystal water. Perhaps mystics of old have seen such places and returned with ideas of purgatory.

The idea that the Dead are in the Hive Mind was bolstered by an experience in a later trip. Unknown to me, my friend's father died suddenly of heart failure the same night I was on a high dose. I had known my friend's dad in life, occasionally chatting with him in his last days. During the trance I suddenly heard old Italian sounding music (the guy was Italian) so clear that I was able to hum the melody into my tape recorder. And lo! There was my friend's dad being carried aloft upon the shoulders of his ancestors in a merry parade. The column of people filed past once and vanished into the Hive.

There is also the fact that I had met Buddhists out There. Now to be a Buddhist, you would have had to have been an earthling at some time. It would follow, in my belief, that these encounters are real, that the Buddhists were passed on from their earthly lives. (Or at the least I was contacting meditating monks somewhere living still—which is just as mind-blowing!)

Trip Six

The Pool of Awareness

Notes 6/10/03: (1500 mg) I saw a man or demigod on a cliff or bank over a lake of green electric/plasma. The fluid in the pool was made up of human awareness. . . .

This was one of a few times that I encountered something like this. I was made to understand that human awareness, a collection of millions(?) of people's consciousnesses were being poured into one place. In this instance, green electric/plasma fluid spilled though fissures in cavelike walls (the cave seemed to be made of the same thought/rock/strata that the old Englishmen had been tunneling through). It was awareness flowing down into a collection pool, which then seemed to flow out again into openings leading deeper into "subterranean" depths. Although I haven't much more to describe with this vision, I can say that it was one of the more indelible memories from all of the trips. This is what got me thinking about the human race as an It and not a We—before I had heard of idealism or immaterialism.

Is the afterlife a place of no souls, no punishment, no egos? Are we, in the end, just a lumbering larva-god—man in the thought-mud staggering in the depths?—the It/Us in unfoldment, startling itself when It stretches and opens its eyes (is born) and forgets It is God once again? Is the way out of the karmic wheel found by those who occasionally intuit their Itness? Is judgment perfected upon itself when It plunges (dies) again and realizes that all injustice done human upon human, It has done to itself? Does It wrestle with itself, sorting in the depths at being Hitler and Gandhi? Do "bad things happen to good people" because of collateral damage? Perhaps It has no rules for growing, no guidelines for a course of action—only the pain/pleasure of becoming, moving, striving for, yet waiting on freedom. . . .

And what will become of It if, when the dust settles, and humans, having come so far, lose the race between greed and spirituality?—when this overpopulated world still half-crazed with religious zeal goes spiraling into extinction? Can the Other help? Is the Hive substantial enough now to remain a part of the cosmic neighborhood without any more human experiences to add to its collection of knowledge? The Hive seems ready to go on. Homo sapiens, however, are clearly in danger . . . we are in desperate need of help from There or we'll never make it Here!

The Face of God

Notes (Trip Six): The face of god . . . anyone is allowed to inspect it. . . .

What happened was I had entered an area that had the feeling of a stage (there seemed to be an audience—unseen but felt). There were "men" looking at something, discussing the implications of a "thing." I was allowed to float in and circle the discussion. The men turned to me and stepped back so I could see. They had been looking at a tiny speck of dirt(?). They were saying: "Even something so (apparently) insignificant does not go uninspected/judged."

This speck of dirt I realized was again the "thought-mud" . . . the same stuff of the tunneling ancestors. I understood that every human experience, everyone's story, would be told. I don't want to say by the word "judged" that I had any sense that they were implying anything like a biblical hellfire, but I did come away feeling that there is a sorting out. Maybe some egos indeed are poured back into that pool of awareness and, though not erased, scattered.

As I continued to hover over the stage area my attention was drawn again to the doings of the men. They again moved aside and I floated in to see a face. "The face of God," it was explained.

How can this be? I thought.

This face was some kind of ancient mask. *A mask!* It was hollow, like a plastic Halloween mask . . . empty, with holes for eyes. It wasn't until later, when I was able to reflect upon this vision, that I realized what might be the significance of the Mask.

I believe that being shown the Face of God as a mask was to demonstrate that our collective or personal notions of God are whatever we put that mask on. *The face is hollow . . . a shell.*

The Spiral

Notes (Trip Six): I think I've been enlightened!

There is no other explanation. . . .

Earlier, in trip three under "Breaks in Time" I related my experience with what I called "flashovers." I went through a harrowing time, returning to everyday reality every other second, and having to remind myself who I was and what my life meant to me. I said that I had gotten "used to" flashingover, but I did not mean that it was enjoyable. During the first one I was sure I had gone too far and that I might not come back, forever stuck reinventing my life second to second. (Strangely, some part of me calmly thought: *I'll just shoot myself if this doesn't go away.*)

These states, up until trip six, always happened when I got up sometime after the peak, or during it, when I would get off the bed and walk out for a little conversation with my sitter. (I would relate a few things, have a cigarette, and return to the bed and the trance state.)

This time was different.

So far my descriptions of things seen in these states has been, to some degree, accurate—in that, although largely impressions, these descriptions are nonetheless of things I could see. Peripheral though the sights were, I got very good at attuning my Middle Eye to detail. What is lacking in all of this is the *feeling* of it all.

What happened next was visual . . . but its *feel* is utterly unrelatable.

There was a tunnel of greenish light made up of two spirals. These spirals were, as I wrote in my notes, *a puzzle within a puzzle.* The two spirals were opposed. It was yin yang. It was the Secret. It seemed as though there was a man and a woman in the tunnel with me. The man reached out and touched the surface of the dual spirals and they swirled. I desperately tried to grasp the Secret. But the movement of the surface I intuitively knew had erased the "combination" to this "lock." And it was no "lock" like any human can imagine. This "lock" was the Great Tantalizer.

In every psychedelic experience there seems to be always a last minute detail one cannot work out—paradox—always a clause in the contract. This was that paradox, finally standing before me.

To see it, to be in its presence, was enough.

To know that there was indeed such a Secret, lent itself to peace of mind in that, one has to say: *So, there IS a reason for all of this!* I got the impression that even my "hosts" did not know what the "answer" beyond was. I also sensed their mirth at my instinctive attempt to wrap my mind around this and understand what it meant.

Ann Shulgin in the book *PiHKAL,* told of what has been called "The Dissociative Spiral"—something that would sometimes happen to her when she was young, just before sleep. A few trip reports have mentioned it. I can't speak for others, whether they experienced this same thing. Certainly the word "spiral" is apt. But what I saw next was probably the most important thing I will ever see, save the coming of Christ in the clouds.

There was a huge circular gas or plasma cloud (obviously "what" it was I cannot know). It reminded me of a spiral galaxy. Inside, all through the "cloud" were humans! It was people reaching toward each other . . . "peeping" through tunnels, feeling for one another. In the center of the spiral-cloud was what looked like a huge, jagged, brown crystal . . . like a chunk of frozen rootbeer.

As I said, there is no way to relate how I felt as I witnessed this. It was the end of the psychedelic. There was love, hope . . . but there was the uncertainty of the Thing still growing. It was growing toward an end that It itself did not know. It was, beyond a doubt, human awareness. And not the blended awareness like I saw being poured into the Pool. Here was individuals . . . "fingertips" touching through corridors of light . . . "eyes" acknowledging each other, reassuring—"We're making it!"

It was later, when this happened again, that I realized it was the "flashover" event from earlier trips. This was important. In the section "Outposts of Reality" I reported how I was placed back in my body on the bed while some "thing" constructed everyday reality around me—ending with the thing throwing me a wink. I knew that the Spiral was the flashingover because I could *feel* it as the same vitally important event. I say it was important (to connect the flashover with the Spiral) because I had experienced it with eyes open, as well as in a deep trance.

The event was the same, my perspectives different.

To witness the Great Paradox of the Spiral by default there had to be a parting of the Veil of reality. In the closed-eye trip, the view was the Spiral. With eyes open, when this event "hit," there was the intermittent view of everyday reality (the flashover). So, with eyes open, I was witnessing the Paradox still. The Spiral was upon me and I'm certain that if I closed my eyes and relaxed during the "flashover" I would have been at the Spiral. By making the connection between the two, I realized I had seen two views of this Thing. Wildness is everywhere. . . .

Thought Cakes

Notes (Trip Six): I can feel "chunks" of thought
forming themselves together with outside thoughts
. . . like clear cakes of water/plastic.

This phenomenon is a bit harder to explain than some of the others. At a certain time, usually during peak moments, there is a sensation that is felt as the construction of jelly/thought. (I said this wouldn't be easy!) The mind seems to be a part of some growing—of something that is conveyed somehow as connecting with other human minds. It feels like squares of jellylike cakes are joining up and aligning themselves, and these cakes are thought. I instantly thought of the Princeton Noonesphere project (where scientists are trying to confirm, with the use of computers, that there is a single mind at work over the planet—a supermind made up of all the human minds on Earth).

Each time I had this experience, I got the feeling that I was evolving. I was witnessing evolution. Once, while this jelly/thought was forming, I had this profound sensation of pain/pleasure course through my body and mind. I had the tape recorder in my hand and I said in to it: "Evo . . . luuu . . . tion . . . it hurts to change!" I have no doubts that evolution is happening in leaps, in consciousness, and that I was on the leading edge of it during these times. There isn't a lot more to report about this sensation except to say that from this point on, it would happen on every trip.

Trip Seven

More on the Ancestors

Notes 6/11/03: (1500 mg) English ... the
epitome of Englishness. Grinding face-
powder, wooden teeth ... apple, oak? I
went into a vein somewhere way back in
the Hive. It was ancestry again. I saw a
crusty place where all the Wooten line is.
(Wooten is my grandfather's name.)

There were two visions here. The first one was a pow-
erful feeling of Englishness. That is, the mindset of an
Englishman from yesteryear was pervading the vision.
The face-powder, and something to do with applewood
and oak—I'm not sure why—seemed to be important.

The mindset was that of superiority. In their minds,
the English were civilized. Anyone not English was
there to be conquered. The history books don't mention
this. Even if they wanted to dwell on the atrocities of
England's past, historians have only the deeds, which,

telling though they are, seem to loom in our minds as somehow justified. Even American history books are sympathetic when it comes to really telling the story of what England has done in the past. What this vision showed me, and what people in the twenty-first century (at least those who have not had this kind of experience) will never understand, is the almost fanatical thought process of the people who lived in these times.

As I hovered in this place, someone came to me—a personage was near. The whole English mindset of old (which I understood at the time was me, or I came out of it) went tumbling down. The fat, glutinous, hypocritical, powder-face mass of English tyrannical ideals fell into a crevice. The person with me seemed to spit on it. He and I watched the "thing" die. . . . I was growing.

The other vision was a disturbing view of some resting place of my grandmother, and my grandaunts and -uncles. It was a place of their awareness, but also their "bones." They had all been very religious—Christian—and I wonder if their belief systems have rendered them terrified to move. Conspicuously missing from this crusty place was grandfather Wooten—the only one who wasn't a real solid believer in Christ . . . a more philosophical man was he.

This whole business with ancestry is one of the most consistent themes in all of these trip/trances. I have written here of a couple of the more glaring examples. There were many other happenings with ancestry and blood lines all through, though. I am surprised that this has not shown up in any reports. Terence McKenna mentions in *The Archaic Revival* his seemingly intuitive notion that at death one traverses back through the ancestor line into oblivion or some Singularity of All. He might have been on to something.

There are ancestor cults around the world and I now wonder if they, too, are onto something.

In the near-death experience (NDE) it is commonly reported—and I have seen it for myself—that loved ones known in life, and who have since died, are there at the Border to welcome the approaching soul coming their way from this world. There are also others there. When I had my NDE, I saw a throng of people but only my grandmother stood out. The others may well have been relatives I have never met! Here is a different vision that lends itself to that end.

Fabrics of Families

Notes (Trip Seven): There are fabrics of groups of people . . . The Known in the Hive is fabrics of awareness. Families chatting, knitted into a quilt. It was a very clear thing that I sailed over.

And so it was. I could hear/feel the people "talking" in a huge rubbery looking sheet that seemed boundless. I understood it was families of the Dead. There were children "playing," mothers relaxed and resigned to their current place . . . elders and fathers, all taking it easy. The reason for their ease seemed to be their togetherness. Just as in this reality, there seemed to be strength in numbers there. In fact the fabric was a sort of defense. This was yet another time that I was reminded that the Hive is not settled. There is unrest there. People getting stepped on. Should I say . . . there is war? Maybe. There is certainly a growth process going on that is reminiscent of our political and religious struggles on earth. It is the sorting out I made mention of before, in trip six, "The Face of God."

The Machinery Behind

Notes (Trip Seven): I was in the Spiral again! This time I got a different view. . . .

I was standing up after using the bathroom. I was peaking heavily. The Thought Cakes were manifesting. Then, the Spiral hit. I saw it with eyes open. I was on a kind of "chair" made out of the same greenish plasma of the Spiral from before. In front of me people were getting in line and, soon I realized, behind me as well.

This is when it hit me: *This is a technology. Enlightenment is a machine!*

I had the wherewithal to try and study this from as neutral a mindset as I could muster. I thought: *I'm in the animal mind . . . from before we had language. there is no context here. Enlightenment is a discontinuity . . . a program! Reality's being run from Behind!*

What I was seeing was a frozen piece of time. It was a course humans were traversing, but they seemed stuck there—frozen. It was promising enough that there was a Way, a path so to speak, but the feel of it was that, to complete the course, one would be there a long time. Or, my perspective was from outside the whole event, outside of time, which made the "machine" seem frozen. Though I was seeing it as a "path" this time, it was the Spiral . . . the flashingover again.

The feel of this Way as being a program or "machine" was strong. To call it a technology is fitting only in that it is a kind of system—obviously not the nuts-and-bolts kind—I did look for that, too, though! Like everything in the Hive, the "appliances" and "molecules" and even the Crab Faced Other—organic machinery might be the best description. This Machinery Behind, when one thinks about it, is promising.

I am reminded of the "Cambrian explosion" some 530 million years ago, when virtually all major groups of modern animals were quite suddenly here, with a bang, on the scene. The basic anatomies of all presently existing animals, from worms to vertebrates, appeared suddenly, together. (Before the Cambrian, 3.2 billion years passed with life confined to one-celled organisms, or at most, globular forms known as Ediacaran fauna that came about 650 million years ago.) The mystery here is: how did the basic anatomies of all life extant today arise in the twenty or so million years of the Cambrian, out of one-celled protozoans and bacteria? I am not a paleontologist, but Stephen Jay Gould was, and in his book *Wonderful Life* he has made it evident that there was NOT ENOUGH TIME FOR THIS TO HAPPEN! There is nowhere in the strata of rock from the beginning of the Cambrian any organisms remotely hinting at the myriad of body styles found by the end of the Cambrian.

My point?

There is something at work here. Yes, the "C" word—I'm going there—creation. People take everything in this world for granted. The whole set up we have found ourselves in is mind-bendingly ludicrous on every level, but the absurdity of finding ourselves in a body with no explanation is so monstrously strange as to be debilitating. People gather inside the boundaries of the Known and gather toys unto themselves to ward off this most basic mystery. The shunning of this not-knowing is taken further, to include a communal self-convincing of the importance of all things trivial. We convince ourselves that things around us are "normal" and that what's happening has been mostly figured out by somebody who knows about such matters. Even our destiny has been packaged for us in religions! But really, the absolutely astounding is all around us.

None of this is chance.

I saw a program on television, where a scientist made a good case for the emergence of eyes at the time of the Cambrian to be the cause of the sudden diversity that happened. (I forget his name but he was giving Gould's ascertainments a casual shrug.) But again I heard a scientist not tell it all. The story of the emergence of eyes is itself enough for one to give pause. In his book *The Science of God,* Gerald L. Schroeder makes some important points concerning the unlikelihood of what is called *convergent evolution:* "seen in complex body organs when *very different* phyla of animals develop very *similar* organs to satisfy similar needs. Being of different phyla, they have been genetically separated since the inception of multicellular life. Hence, they develop these similar solutions *independently.*" (Italics Schroeder.)

A glaring example is the similarity of the eye of the octopus and that of a human. Each is from a different phyla, and that means no information has passed between the two (mollusks and mammals) since each was a single-celled animal at the beginning of the Cambrian!

Says Schroeder: "Mollusca and vertebrates, as with all the thirty-four animal phyla, separated 530 million years ago, at the developmental level just above protozoa. Yet their solutions to the need for sight are almost identical. . . . The statistical improbability of pure chance yielding even the simplest forms of life has made a mockery of the theory that random choice alone gave us the biosphere we see."

In his book *Darwin's Black Box,* Michael J. Behe explains that the likelihood of even the "simplest" life form, i.e., a single-celled algae, stirring to life suddenly in a pool of backwater, is less than that of an internal combustion engine being produced on a mountainside by the forces of wind and rain. Simple life forms are anything but simple. And when I say "suddenly" stirring to life . . . that's what it would have to be.

Every tiny piece of machinery inside a cell is an irreplaceable part of a huge *cascading system* where, if just one component is missing the thing isn't alive. Remember the game called "Mouse Trap"? As the game unfolded, each player would put into place a plastic part in a linear path on the game board. The turn of a handle and a marble fell, causing a man to fly from a ramp into a bucket, which caused something else to move, etcetera. That is a cascade of action. All of the parts have to be in place, ALL AT ONCE, for the action to reach from the beginning to the end—or, for a cell to become something living. A cell is either alive, with the whole supercomplex system in place, or it is dead (never was alive!) with just one tiniest of parts missing. For a cell to evolve by the random bumping of molecules, there would have to be at some point in time, a thing, outrageously complex, with ninety-nine percent of its parts in place, just laying around "unalive," waiting for that last piece—itself a piece absolutely "custom-made" for the job—to arrive and bolt itself onto the system. (Think of a car engine with no spark plugs.) That is the difference between one nanosecond and the next.

There is Machinery Behind.

This is peculiar "machinery" though. It can self-replicate. It is full of mind-from-within. It is expanding in the Deep, building more of itself through some secret blueprints—blueprints that are created as they are followed. The Mind of God (and I don't mean a judge in the sky) *is* pure paradox. All might be thought of as creatorless creation. Intent discovered itself, ambition was born. A potential for destination emerged. The It shook itself awake! We are the fall-out. . . .

The chaos theorists tell us that self-organization crops up in everything, all the time. What is called *iteration* is basically feedback loops . . . the continual reabsorption, by a system, of what has just happened in that system. (It could be *any* system, from weather to cells dividing.) Order leaps from chaos. But there needs to be both chaos and order (uncertainty and destination) for either to exist. It is the yin yang. Paradox *is* the Answer. (Check out *Turbulent Mirror* by John Briggs and F. David Peat. This book takes the layperson right to the edge of this strange topic without losing them.)

The Circus Behind

Notes (Trip Seven): There was a carnival-like mosaic . . . very psychedelic. I wondered if the word "psychedelic" wasn't standing in the way of our

concept of what is Behind reality—that we have
been conditioned to think of the kaleidoscopic
weirdness as somehow silly and unreal . . . when in
fact it is precisely what there is to be found in some
other dimensions.

In his book *DMT: The Spirit Molecule,* Rick Strassman, M.D.,
wrote the accounts of his brave subjects who were adminis-
tered high doses of DMT. In the notes it is immediately obvious
that these people were going to the same "places" . . . laboratories of "alien" beings, high-tech labyrinthine vaulted areas,
sometimes with cartoonish or clownlike beings present. This is
striking. Dr. Strassman himself had to conclude in the end that
actual contact with some Other must have happened. (I would
like to say that Dr. Strassman's willingness to write about his
struggles and doubts on many levels, from political to personal,
as well as those endured by the volunteers, is absolutely com-
mendable. What he was able to do—convince people in high
places, in a time when commercials about drug abuse bombard
us daily, to let him have a batch of DMT and shoot-up people
with it—is amazing!—and yet somewhat overlooked in the psychedelic community.)

At the time of this writing I haven't yet smoked any DMT.
I would like to, especially to compare the "machinery" and
beings described by the DMT explorers with what I have seen
on DXM. I get the feeling that these "places" are, if not the
same, at least nearby neighborhoods.

What I saw was a stained glass looking wall. It was shimmering with multicolored light. On this wall was a moving figure
like a clown. Immediately I thought: *It's the DMT clown!* What

could this mean, this sighting of clowns? After much reflection on the clown phenomenon I began to see it as expression. As with the Dream Chamber, I got the feeling that it took on a carnivalesque feel only because I was conditioned to think of that image as silly. But to the purpose of existence, which, as my suspicions hold, may be no more than experience/expression—a look around for the It/Us, with purpose, at least initially, coming about by degrees as the potential for purpose arises—silly works as well as serious. Expression is like chaos theory, where order manifests out of seemingly unordered states of things. In other words, the Silly exchanges glances with the Serious, and one is no more important to the emergence of the self-aware universe than the other. Both need to be, for either to even be recognizable. Drama is everything in the end.

I keep emphasizing: All is Wilderness. This is what I mean. To go into these other realities with the mindset of a naturalist is to accept what might be, not what is hoped will be found.

Somewhere in the world somebody is being tortured and in a house around the corner a kid is telling a joke to his buddy.

People may not like this idea. Why though, should we think of the nonphysical realms as a place where a division of good and evil lies? Eternal damnation in hellfire is not much drama when you think about it—neither is a heavenly realm of endless tranquillity. This is not to say, though, that neighborliness is not now the goal of the It/Us . . . it's just that it may be a new goal, one of happenstance. The monkeyman has created purpose finally. A distinction between wildness and civility has become valid to the emerging expression seeking It. Also, there seems to be human alliances affording places of reflection and stability to be found over There. The trip/trance has revealed many such "dwellings."

(I have experienced some events that seem to show that awareness—the sense of there being a "me"—may in some cases be "allowed" to continue after death. It may be an every man/woman for themselves situation though. I hate to say this, but It may want to keep the illusion of the "me" state for some It deems worthy. The rest—humans and animals alike—might be scattered in the Pool of Awareness . . . not truly unmade as I have said, but blended into the pot, perhaps for another shot at being an organism.)

Trip Eight

The Next Level

This journey was the first indication that I might be able to induce the Spiral experience. It was done by entering into one of the shinier crevices that would sometimes appear. The object was to single these out. Inside there would be something going on . . . "appliances" doing things in "apartments" and such. But in the distance, if I didn't give my attention to the "room" at hand, I would notice still another shiny crevice and move toward it. Into this I would go, passing through tight, almost claustrophobic areas filled with transparent or pink tubes that gave the feeling of an underground self-running scientific laboratory.

Then, in a flash I would be There. The man and

woman from before were there too, near the Spiral. This time I was disorientated somewhat, like I was turned away from the Spiral itself. I heard the woman say, "He's reached the next level." She seemed surprised that I had made it so far.

I am not trying to give myself a pat on the back here. This statement by the woman, while certainly promising to me, or at least my ego, is as well something for everybody. The Idea that there is achievement to be made, and that it is recognized over There, needs no elaboration of its importance by me. There may well be a merit system in place.

Offers of Power

Notes (Trip Eight:) There are people in a wood/clay mass. They move, here and there, popping up and settling down again . . . merging into the wood/clay. They ARE the wood/clay. As I pass over I can hear/feel them "calling" to me. They seem wondrous that I can fly. They want me to lead them!

This was one of many times I had the sensation that there was power to be had in the Hive. It was political power, not some kind of magic. Each time I ignored these offers because I felt that it was either a trap, or that I didn't know what saying "Yes, I will help" might entail.

Notes: I saw a giant glowing orb of light. I understood that it was power. It represented Pure Truth. But it couldn't be wielded for long. For the first time

some "thing" mentioned Christ or his equivalent.
It was saying, "It is not that the power corrupts the
one who carries it so much as the followers mistrust
that one no matter what . . . therefore the power
changes hands, is endlessly passed on."

I sighed at the problem of power. I was thinking: *It's what makes things go . . . but it is a shame that it can't be used in one way, for good things.*

Then this Other said something like: Power is of perception, of circumstance . . . a course of events under its perceived presence. It exists in numbers of beings as it has to. It must continuously leak in one place even as it rises and manifests somewhere else.

Trip Nine

Losing Humanness

Notes 8/1/03: (1300 mg) At the mirror . . . I saw myself as an alien.

In one fell moment during a bathroom run, I discovered the source of the isness or suchness that pervades psychedelic states. This "zen stink" is the imbued significance that "sticks" to everything and anything one lays their eyes on under the influence of any psychedelic. There is an electric realness to the world and the objects in it.

What happened at the mirror was not the typical morphing of the face, taking on identities or melt, etc., so commonly reported, especially with LSD. No, my face was perfectly in focus. I knew it was my same old face. But I saw it as a strange face—it was the face of a stranger. It was deeper than this though. I saw my form as a galactic foreigner. The idea that that face was mine seemed like a dream. The deep conditioning that had caused the relaxed belief in that face was mine, or even the idea that I had ever accepted being human . . . accepting that roll, was suddenly lifted and it all seemed like a crazy idea.

I thought: *This is what suchness is! To trace suchness to its source is to lose one's humanness. I was never a human before this . . . I'm not from Here, I'm from over There!*

This was more profound than I can relate. I believe now that the "sticky" zen-stink-suchness is a glimpse of the world from a phase-shifted line of sight. It is the cracks in the Matrix . . . the leaky valve—the snake finding its tail and realizing it is not a snake. Beyond that valve is the nonhuman source. The brain in the mind, the mind somewhere in the Deep—Behind.

We are not humans. This is a play . . . drama for the sake of drama, things done because they can be. It was bored, no?

Trip Ten

Contacting the Dead

> Notes 8/20/03: (1200 mg) I wasn't expect-
> ing this, but it seems I'm able to dial up my
> deceased loved ones!

It is with some reluctance that I report this. I am skeptical of this kind of stuff—mediums on television who,
in a matter of seconds, start to describe a person's dead
grandfather say, by a process of elimination: "I see a
man in a hardhat. Did your grandfather ever wear a
hardhat? Yes? Okay he's here in the room . . . he's telling me . . . " and so on. I wouldn't have believed what I
am about to share before the experience, but here it is,
as it went down. . . .

I had been out all night with an acquaintance and got
talked into a few lines of cocaine (something I hadn't
done in a few years). In the wee hours on a Sunday morning I lay awake in bed wired and feeling disappointed in

myself. I thought: *I'll have some DXM to take the edge off.* As I have said, DXM is an anesthetic and twisted though it may be, I force-tripped to try and power into sleep after a ride into the Hive. I did 800 mg. As was my new method, I began to read while waiting for the trip. This kept me from overthinking what I was about to endure.

I had just picked up *Chaos, Creativity, and Cosmic Consciousness* by Rupert Sheldrake, Terence McKenna, and Ralph Abraham, and I was poring over it slowly, as the DXM sped into my brain.

The words began their familiar suchness. The pages and the words took on a holiness. McKenna was saying something about the "Gaian Mind . . . the galactic mind." Then something descended on me, into me, through me. I thought: *Who is reading these words?* I was trying to get my mind around the words "galactic mind." Then the words broke from the page . . . (galactic mind) ((galactic mind)) (((galactic mind))). . . .

Here the dialogue wasn't in English, but if it had been, it would have went something like this. . . .

Me: "Something big is happening! And I gotta piss!"

Other: "We'll try and show you quickly then. You might want to hold it though."

I enter a laboratory. It's the Hive but a part I've never seen. The detail is exquisite. Elaborate detail. I fly over little lights/ beings at work on a blue machine. They are saying: "Hello! Hello! See our work we love to do?" Then I'm over a river of molten glass, clear as air.

Me: "Living water!"

Other: "Something like that perhaps."

I float past other workers. There is a device, another "appliance" of sorts but more important than the earlier ones. It is made of silver fire. No time to look.

Other: "See? Down there . . . " I look and there is a tide of babies. Human babies. They don't look like the human form. They are the "wood/clay" things from before—the Dead.

Me: "They are dead, recently dead?"

Other: "Yes. This person is in charge as they come in. . . . " There is a man overwhelmed by the influx.

Man: "See what comes up? They are confused but not scared." We move on.

Other: "See? Down below. . . . "

I look. "Docking bays? Are those people? Coming in? Going out?"

Other: "Both." (I see there are humans, apparently unconscious being "readied.") We move on.

Other: "See this? Your mind and body." I look. There is a "valve" with millions(?) of tiny lights. They want to communicate but the valve isn't working right. Information is "clogged" at the site.

Other: "They want to know if you want to open communication."

Me: "Yes! Let them talk." (The valve opens and the lights intertwine.)

My friend Beth, who trip sat me in the early days (remember her from the section "Breaks in Time"?) died during the writing of this book. I ask, "Where is Beth?" As I do, I picture her face, think of her voice. There is movement.

Other: (Not talking to me.) "Can we bring her up?"

Different Other: "She is . . . here." (?) I am in a chamber. Feeling is low, far "underground." Beth is hiding alone in a "corner" in fear. I say: "Beth! Beth it's me!" She is dazed. Isn't sure. Two figures come and pick her up, remove her. My attention turns to two young black men. One says: "She's lucky. Someone loves her. Able to come here. We have to start all over. Learn much." I drift away. . . .

My cousin Lynn also died during the writing of this book. I picture him, his voice rings in my head. Movement again. I'm in a hall—it's Lynn's place. He seems startled at my presence, as if it might be a trick. He says: "Danny. I've been doing this." I look at what seems to be art work. I drift away. He's saying, "I love you!"

Me: "I love you!"

Later I come across Beth again in a more bright, friendlier setting. She realizes it really is me. She's saying, "Oh Danny! Danny! I love you so much! We are friends forever."

Me: "Yes! We are! I love you. Now be filled with wonder! Don't be afraid. Learn to wonder . . . be filled with wonder . . ." I drift away. . . .

I am taken to a place where people such as myself, who have had such a tour, are being "processed." My turn comes and my being is "cored." What was a blob (me) has been hollowed out now like a donut—without a middle. I understand it is an honor. It comes with the price of no return (to the old me). I have carte blanche in the Hive Mind now. . . .

I float toward the edges of the Hive.

Other: "These areas you will be able to work in." I look at endless blue "apartments" unused—laboratories full of organic/plasma "machinery." The Other continues: "These are your helpers." I look and a field of swarming lights—tiny knowing orbs drift about me.

The tour is ending. A "gate" closes. The knowing lights are moving behind it. They are saying cheerfully, "Good-bye! Good-bye! Good-bye."

Other: "Do not do cocaine anymore! Good-bye."

Me: "Thank You!"

As I drift to the fringes of the Hive, there are emotions, drifting, unattached—mixed up personalities . . . bits of awareness. I see a family, a man and wife and kids. They are swirling on a merry-go-round of sorts. I join them briefly. I say: "Is this death?"

"Yes!" (They seem resigned to the fact.)

In the evening many hours later, I woke up. I grabbed the twenty-dollar piece of coke my acquaintance had left me, and a cigarette. I went out onto the porch and threw the coke into the wooded lot next to the house and looked up at the night sky . . . The Hive! I could still see it, eyes open! The whole thing stretching out before me swirling: Taffy-Clouds, the Knowing Lights, orbs, Plasma Flowers. . . . I thought of Beth and cried.

Then my roommate appeared on the adjacent porch a few yards away. In the darkness she couldn't tell my state. My cat came nudging up to me. I said: "I don't think I'm gonna get him fixed. He's taken to living in the box I made. He can't come inside now that he sprays . . . grown up."

A conversation about stray pets followed.

Suddenly a poodle came out of the night across the lawn. (We live about three miles outside of Levittown, Pennsylvania where the corn fields begin—the dog was lost.) He came straight over to me. "Hey Helen. There's a tag with a phone number on him."

"Cool. Here, I'll take him. Wow! What a coincidence!"

"I guess." (A half-hour later the owner shows up and takes the dog home.)

I went back inside saying under my breath: "Synchronicity. . . . Home."

The Invisible
Landscape

As I write these words, nine months have passed since trip ten. Much in the way of solidifying my theories about existence and what can be detected in the psychedelic trance has occurred during that time. There have been three more big trips since, and I estimate that I have spent about one hundred hours in the Hive by now. And always I find the *same* things . . . rooms, appliances, beings—the Dead! Let's pick up now on what further observations I have made . . . back into the quest shall we? Before we go straight into the reports though, I want to reevaluate some things. All of these descriptions of things seen in the closed-eye trance are maddeningly hard to pin down. As in the area of say: *what's brain?* and *what's Other?*

In the early days all was new, and I wasn't sure that *anything* I was seeing was "outside" of me. Inner space, outer space, was there even a difference? Well, no; it was beginning to seem to me that despite the glaring problem of not knowing how or why we humans got here (or more creepily, as it becomes when you ponder the fact that you are alone, always have been, and will be as you toss in the failing flesh in that strange hour, years or minutes ahead, when it is time to exit the body), I had seen much to enforce this growing idea of some It Behind—a blind groping hand of "God" reaching from Behind the soup of atoms and up the DNA strands to feel its created self in the Here.

Room One

In the beginning stages of the DXM trip, when the eyes are closed and things are quiet, there stirs in the peripheral field aside the mind's eye—that third eye of the mystics—yellow/green lines of churning light. This taffiness morphs itself into semisquare "wood" panels . . . thick leathery electric Doors. They are "shut" . . . motionless at first. I have been to these Doors many times. The squared-off shapes infer some Mind Behind. (I feel at times awkward, floating as a dissociative particle.) This area I call Room One. It contains as well many aware, shape-shifting plastic/plasma formations. After so much study, I have concluded that these Room One residents are likely some kind of "theater" props for dreaming. The experience of the Dream Chamber may be linked to this "shallow" area. At times I am fooled into believing that I am seeing some spatial distance . . . Rome 100 A.D. with columns of marching soldiers, sunlight glistening off their helmets—only to take another look and realize it's the shapeshifting plasma I am looking at!

Behind the Doors some Other must sense my presence. The Doors begin to bubble as I float before them. Soon they glide apart and I pass. Chambers and passageways of living Hive

open up. New, more machine-feeling plastic red, yellow, pink
. . . tubes, orbs, and wormy light-beings follow (the Plasma
Flowers). These days I just say, "Hey guys, nice night for floating about?" and I slip down, out, into the Deep.

Machine Elves Solved

During the preceding year when Beth was still alive, I enjoyed a
naive time of exploration . . . thoughtless of my extreme luck at
having such a great friend as she was to sit for me. It was during those carefree days when I had a vision, which would later
turn out to be central in my theories—namely concerning those
little beings I had been agonizing over . . . the Plasma Flowers,
and "molecules," etcetera.

I came out of the bedroom late in the morning, tape recorder
in hand, wrapped in my favorite blanket.

Beth said: "Did we have an interesting time? Want coffee?"

"Yes and yes," I said. "You got a piece of paper, too? And
where are my colored markers?"

I drew a picture of something I had seen deep in-trance the
night before. It was a series of "plastic" tubes linked together.
"With electron-looking things coming into it," I explained to
Beth when I had finished the picture. "It was made of thought
is the only way I can explain its design . . . or what it was.
And these electrons-things were *instructions* pouring into the
tubes."

Beth took one long look and said, "That looks like DNA!"
And it did.

Not for the first time, I concluded that I was seeing on a
molecular level. That day I went looking for books on DNA and
found a few in the local library. Right away it became apparent

that the writers were down the same path as neuroscience—nobody was willing to admit that; THIS STUFF IS MINDED. (At this point of course, I feel it's preposterous to think of consciousness as being the result of random events in a tidal pool eons ago.) At the time of the DNA vision, I was just beginning to give up on science books about the brain, and the biology books now too had begun to lose me.

So it was that, with so many other awesome experiences to assimilate into my belief system, I soon forgot about the DNA experience. In fact, how could I be sure that it was DNA I had seen? Intuitively it felt true, but what more could I do? I didn't write about it until now . . . that there's been some outside corroboration—namely by the anthropologist Jeremy Narby in his book *The Cosmic Serpent*.

This book may well be one of the most important books ever written!

Briefly stated, Narby is apparently the first person to grasp the significance of *ladders, ropes, vines, bridges,* and *chains,* etc.—seen in visions and commonly referred to by shamans on all five continents, as being *links* between heaven and earth. Narby had a eureka moment while reading Mircea Eliade's *Shamanism: Archaic Techniques of Ecstacy*. In that book, Eliade had carried the ball most of the way before dropping it . . . whereupon Narby picked it up for the touchdown. What Mircea had missed, and I assume many scientists are not prepared to talk about, is that these *links* to heaven that the shamans are talking about—in Australia, Tibet, Nepal, Ancient Egypt, Africa, North and South America—is DNA! The symbol of intertwining serpents (the double helix!) is prevalent in the art among these shaman, too. Even in Siberia, where there are no snakes, the shaman have twisting serpents sewn into their garments.

After reading *The Cosmic Serpent,* it was obvious that I had reached the same conclusion as Narby, perfectly independently, through the use of a psychedelic—and that one *does* see on a molecular level in the closed-eye trip/trance!

Now I was to take the ball for a run of my own. . . .

I have mentioned the "self-transforming machine elves" earlier, but it's time to consider them in more detail here. The term was coined by the late great, self-appointed "mouthpiece of the Logos" and psychedelic guru, Terence McKenna. From the interview in Charles Hayes' book *Tripping,* McKenna describes the Machine Elves: "From the moment you enter into the DMT experience, you're in a domain (where) they've been waiting for you. The toys they offer, these *Fabergé eggs,* (messenger RNAs?) are in a sense nothing more than the *plastic geometric shapes* that you would hang over a bassinet. . . . " He goes on: "These entities (the machine elves) seem to be *syntactical creatures made of language."* (Italics mine.)

Now check out Narby's description of the words biologists are forced to use, despite their avoidance of the subject of any meaning behind this most profound of mysteries:

> DNA is a *text,* or a *program,* or *data,* containing *information,* which is *read* and *transcribed* into *messenger*-RNAs. (The ribosomes) are *molecular computers* . . . they *build* the rest of the cell's *machinery* . . . the proteins and enzymes, which are *miniaturized robots.* . . . (All italics Narby's.)

Narby goes on explaining the job of proteins:

> Like versatile marionettes, or jacks-of-all-trades, (the proteins) twist, fold, and stretch into the shape their task

requires (like carrying single atoms to precise places!). What is known, precisely, about these self-assembling machines?

"Self-assembling machines" sounds much like "self-transforming machine elves"!

The Cosmic Serpent came out in 1998 and the above McKenna interview was from January 17 and 18 of 1998. McKenna had already been throwing around the term "self-transforming machine elves" for years by this time, and it would seem unlikely that he would have read *The Cosmic Serpent* by January 17th, if indeed the book was out so early in 1998. Besides if McKenna had read Narby, which doesn't seem likely, he would have surely put two and two together.

I think McKenna was doing all one man could in attempting to figure out *what* these "elves" were. Here is a post I put up on Breakingopenthehead.com, before I had read *The Cosmic Serpent*. I missed the mark myself, thinking these things were tied in with the Ego Vortex. But as you will see, I was dancing around with the idea that McKenna's "world" of DMT beings was in fact the molecular view one can attain in the trip/trance. From Breakingopenthehead.com's message board, February 1, 2004, under *The Dimensional Shift*, titled *Bugs on Bugs:*

> A theory on the consciousness/brain paradox by way of observation in the trip/trance state. I had been witness to a particular event on many occasions in the trip/trance, but never grasped the significance of what I was seeing. I am referring to the "alive, aware parts . . . looking back at me."
>
> These parts HAD to be on a molecular level and of

the brain. This was no illusion or hallucination or blurry, hurried impression/vision. My state was, like reports from people who've smoked DMT, not very psychedelic really. It was perfectly in focus and *there*.

There were times when I would watch this action for 45 minutes at a time . . . so long that the gravity of watching these melting Lego-beings (machine elves?) slice little pieces of themselves off, to create emotions and other information, was lost in boredom.

(This has to be the machine elves. McKenna may have missed something by not investigating DXM—namely that the machine elf world appears to be self/brain.) So these Lego-beings would shave parts of themselves off and others, sensing this, would shave parts of themselves off as well. Then whole groups (thousands?) of these Lego-beings (melting, connecting "Lego" brand children's building blocks for bodies) would be poised to join the slicing, but the consensus wouldn't hold. With no reason to continue, they'd regroup, hovering, slicing, merging.

To show how this was coming together for me, here is some of a post I put up at Breakingopenthehead.com, just after reading Narby posted March 4, 2004 under *Elemental Beings* titled *Machine Elves Solved!:* "Looks like Narby beat me to the punch but dig . . . this is corroboration! I saw DNA, I know it. And the proteins ARE the shape-shifters (machine elves)."

Trip Eleven

The Sprite

Notes 5/13/04: (1000 mg) Well it happened.

. . . I've had my first elf encounter.

I will describe the trip leading up to the encounter because it is a cautionary tale with an important ditch-medicine tip for any who would mix opiates and DXM.

I took a four month break from tripping. This is always a good idea—the brain can certainly use it. A break is also good for the unforeseen connections in working theories that always manifest when the searcher returns to the ego and its grip on consensus reality (the serotonin hallucination!).

But I was starting to be unable to remember the feel of all that enlightenment. I wanted to go big again. My ego was starting to say: *Do we really reckon that Hive Mind to be there after all?* As with my out-of-body experiences in my midthirties, the impact of all these most

Extra-Ordinary visions were, incredibly, ever being undermined by the Pure Ego.

I laid out two 500 mg piles and stirred one into a glass of orange juice and drank. In thirty minutes I did the same again. 1000 milligrams hitting my brain nearly all at once like that was, by now, a manageable ride for me. This time though, either from having taken time off and losing any tolerance I might have gained, or the psychedelic deciding to knock my elitist mindset down a notch, the trip came on big.

(The cautionary part comes in here.) Once, on an earlier trip, I noticed that my leg and stomach muscles had stiffened up considerably more than usual. What is called the "robo shuffle," among the cough syrup-drinking youth, is the way one is forced to walk while on higher doses of DXM . . . because the leg muscles seem to get conflicting signals from the brain— "Move! No stop! Move/stop!" That particular trip I had been unable to secure any benzodiazepines, which I like to use along with DXM for a steadying effect—my rudder in big waters (valium is my first choice but xanax will do). What I did use was a couple of opiates (percocet) instead.

Opiates can cramp the muscles, as is noticeable in the way one can hardly move one's bowels while on them. DXM by itself, too, causes sometimes severe muscle problems and I reasoned that I had had a reaction, a doubling effect of the two drugs. (In fact during the early trips, I would secure plenty of water and keep a bucket next to the bed for urinating because of these muscle problems that could render me virtually immobile during peak hours. I could move if there was an emergency but it was uncomfortable.) Now, on the trip I'm reporting here, I had used opiates again, ignoring the warnings to myself from before.

✳

So the trip came on big. Soon my legs stiffened up—locked up is more like it. I couldn't bend them. I felt that I might throw a convulsion. About this time I realized I only had one sixteen-ounce bottle of water. In the huge farmhouse I rent with my brother and one friend, my bedroom is on one far end of the place, at the basement level. Nobody would hear me if I called out and climbing the stairs was impossible. I tried to get out of bed and slunk to the floor. In the semidark, my hand bumped into the grocery bag I had put there earlier that day . . . a six-pack of V8 juice! (A lucky break that certainly saved me from a bad trip as I was still six long, thirsty hours away from base-line.) So with my lower half in full paralysis, I tried to get into the trip on the floor. I began to see things, eyes open, before me.

First came a tunnel that opened up about a foot in front of my face. It was a "device" of some sort, "made" for looking through . . . plasma binoculars if you will. I put my face up to the thing. A voice said I was to be given "secrets." For a time I beheld some vast expanse. It was a region of electricity, of great crystals towering below a ceiling of light. Liquid effervescent light dripped from on high in great knowing rivers of thought. There was a mighty presence that knew I was watching. Unsure of what else to do, I bowed down before this sight. I feel silly about it now, but at the time it seemed natural.

My eyes now away from the "binoculars," I laid back on the floor. Whatever was there—some Otherness—wasn't finished with me. It began to speak: "All self-awareness is chance. All sentientness in the universe arises to discover itself purely by virtue of circumstance in the cloud of atoms that is everything, the stars and planets. . . ." As I was told this, I understood, too, that the Origin that imparts Itself into the cloud of atoms is absolutely *not* of chance.

I was frozen on my side, legs like boards, and a new vision descended. The paneled wall of the room became a forest. From it emerged a "witch" (the feeling was of a female demigod). She was laughing and definitely zeroing in on me—and getting a kick out of my situation! Then she said: "Comes the sprite!"

I thought: *Sprite? Wha . . . ?*

Daniel Pinchbeck wrote: "Once you have seen the elves, you might as well trepan your skull to complete the process."

Well, pass me the drill.

From out of the forest came an elflike creature about one foot tall! It was gray with long, skinny fingers. It came up to my side and hugged my lower right leg. It said: "You are rare among humans . . . born of the moon. The trees send their regards!" (I understood that it was talking about the time when I was tripping in some woods by my house and I had communed with some old trees, touching them and talking to them. I was sure that they knew I was there.) The sprite went on: "This was placed with you on your birth as you came through. . . ." Here the sprite was referring to the spot on the back of one's skull where the hair twirls to a point. It was saying that this spot is where human awareness enters the embryo in the womb.

The odd thing here was the witch's use of the word "sprite." I realize I must have read that word, as it was used to describe a pixie or elf, somewhere in my past . . . but I really can't say. Until this experience I had never used it in a sentence. I was uncertain enough as to whether it was more than just the name of a soft drink that I had to look it up in the dictionary the next day—half expecting it to not be there—it was: "an elf, fairy, or goblin" according to Webster. Soon after I looked through a few books on elves in a bookstore and found that the sprite is traditionally thought of as having to do with the forest. . . . "The trees send their regards," the sprite had said.

Trip Twelve

Astral Projection

Notes 6/2/04: (1100 mg) I was deep in-trance when I began to tumble. I braced myself as I was catapulted forward by what felt like a gust of wind. I had a vision . . . there was a woman saying to someone else, "He has noticed us . . . ." (?) For whatever reason I found myself thinking: This is proof of an afterlife! I opened what I thought were my physical eyes but found myself floating along my bedroom ceiling.

I told of my out-of-body experiences (OBEs) here and there in this book. I wasn't sure if I would go into more detail about them because the OBEs before this one had all happened without the use of any drugs, and so the subject seemed perhaps more geared for another book. Now it has happened on the psychedelic and this gives me good reason to go over my history with this phenomenon.

That a person's awareness can leave the physical body is an immensely important fact. If more people knew this firsthand (despite what they say about their faith) the happier the fabric of society would be.

One day in the fall of 1996, I was thumbing through a pile of used books in a thrift shop and came upon Robert Monroe's *Journeys Out of the Body*. It was a lifechanging happenstance that cost fifty cents! I went home and read the book in two days. Monroe described a vibrational state that occurs prior to the actual separation of consciousness from the body, in which the body feels like an electrical current is passing through it, minus the pain. A month or so after finishing the book I began to have these vibrations, along with intense roaring or hissing in my ears, usually in the morning as I lay still, just after waking. I can only speculate that the reading of Monroe's book itself opened my mind to the idea that people were really having OBEs and so afforded the conditions through which I was able to leave my body. In the notes from 1997 I described the experiences as "fever episodes" because the sensation reminded me of a time in my childhood when I had a high fever. Nine months after reading Monroe's book I recorded this lucid dream that sums up nicely what I was going through and how I was beginning to sort out what I believed.

Dream log 8/30/97: I was floating—levitating
over and around Mom's house. Debbie emerges
and seeing me, asks what I am doing. I start to
go straight up—the dream now lucid. I say: "I'm

going up into space." As I rose I could see the Milky Way. The stars grew close together so that it seemed I was far into the galactic core. Then at least two "fever episodes" occurred. I foolishly moved my head on one and a noise in the house had arrested the other. Note: The episodes were definitely connected to the lucid dream. This particular fever was very strong. In case I don't wake from one of these episodes, I will describe what is happening. Sometime just after a lucid dream . . . a sort of pressure builds in my head and my heart rate seems to climb . . . but then it's lost (the sense of feeling my own heart beat) because the body becomes numb. The head starts to swim in a sort of fever—all the while there is a pressure, but not like a weight. A fever without the sickness might be close. I can only guess that I'm breaking through . . . somehow slipping through, bypassing the dream filter—perhaps the early stages of projecting. As of 8/29/97 I'm still not completely sure but I sense it's something real and big and rare.

I was amazed around this time when I looked over a dream log from 1982 and found this account: *Driving with Bob, flying off a cliff. I said: "It's been nice knowing you." Then I woke up. I felt like I had a fever.*

Around the same time (1982) I unwittingly induced the vibrations while sitting up awake. At the time I did not have a knowledge of lucid dreaming—never mind that leaving the body was possible. I was playing around with the idea that my consciousness might be inhabiting my body in a way similar to that of a hand slipped into a glove. I imagined that my arms were indeed long gloves or gauntlets and I began to mentally pull out of them. As I did this the vibrations came on. I panicked and leapt from my bed and ran out to the living room to watch television until late. I wouldn't understand what I had done until fifteen years later.

In his book *A Crack in the Cosmic Egg*, Joseph Chilton Pierce wrote convincingly of the sway our belief system can have over what is or is not possible in the universe. In short, he is saying how seemingly incredulous feats, which might bother our precepts of reality or threaten our sense of logic on some level, are actually possible, once these "impossibilities" are given an open-minded consideration by our belief system. These feats will then manifest and come to be and our current reality will be changed into a new reality. This seems to have been the case for me in regard to OBEs. Conquering fear of the unknown and being open to the possibility of astral travel is apparently all one need do for results. (With all things considered I do believe that keeping a dream log, which led to lucid dreaming, was the first step.)

Before I was ever truly out of my body, I had a series of partial projections. These were experiences where it seemed part of my body, a leg or an arm, felt like it was reaching up through the blankets that covered me.

Dream log 3/3/97: During sleep intense vibrations occurred. I started to seperate. (I think.) I believe my arms (second body arms) were held straight up through the covers.

I read from Monroe that the second body, now commonly called the astral body, is shaped just like one's real physical body, at least at first. But I was not thinking about what my shape should be as I reached out of my physical. It was perfectly natural and unquestioned that my phantom arms would have the same dimensions as my "real" arms. And so they did. A case of Pierce's intending intent? Maybe. In later OBEs I seemed to have been a point or an orb, usually while traveling.

> Dream log 6/1/97: A semifever came and I felt my
>
> arms peeling out of my physical . . . tried to lift out
>
> but woke momentarily and the fever left.

This is how it began for me. Though it seemed I was popping out of my body somewhat, I still had not, to my unequivocal satisfaction, proven to myself that I was doing anything more than dreaming. Even though it was exactly as Monroe had described it, my experience with the vibration/hiss had not yet convinced me that it was a gateway to the OBE. Speculation turned to concrete belief when I finally had my first real OBE.

> Dream log 12/17/97: Vibrations. Got up to use the
>
> bathroom, came back and laid down. Vibrations
>
> began strong—suddenly there is a "pop." I'm out of
>
> my body—fully conscious! Not thinking, I try to get
>
> up—this puts me in a place with others—people;
>
> some women working at something. I try to com-
>
> municate by saying hi and waving. They seem

indifferent or mildly annoyed. Then later I'm in bed (don't recall coming back). Vibrations (acid fever) again strong. Again a "pop." This time I twisted out. Totally calm. I knew what had happened—it felt natural. I seemed to be only a few feet above my bed, about six feet off the ground. I tried to look at myself but all I could see was my black quilt—from above! (I sleep with a pillow over my eyes). So it is that I have conclusively projected for the first time on this date.

One thing that stood out right a way was how "natural" the process felt. It is difficult to relate so ineffable a sense as the way I mean "natural." From the feeling as one breaks out of the flesh, to the realization later that the process wasn't forced or dangerous and that the gateway out of the body has been there all along hits home. This gateway is not a way created by the attempt at projecting but is a preexisting certainty that must be included now for those so indoctrinated into the new reality that includes OBE. It felt natural because it did not feel as though I had broken any rules or cheated reality. It was as if there were was an unused tunnel in reality, and when I noticed it, reality said, "Okay. You can go down that tunnel too!"

Having an OBE is unmistakable to the person who has one. When I am out of the body but near it, there is an intuitive sense of where "I" am. When I first began having OBEs, I could not always see my surroundings, but I knew that I was "a few feet above my bed" during the first one. I have not had an

OBE in years as I write this. For whatever reason they stopped happening to me. Here is a list of the OBEs that followed this first one.

> Full projection: 6/18/98, 6/30/98, 10/5/98, 11/2/98,
> 2/11/99, 3/16/99, 7/6/99, 9/8/99, 10/18/99,
> 10/25/99, 11/5/99, 11/24/99, 12/30/99, 1/11/00,
> 9/23/01, 10/12/01, 10/23/01, 11/28/01, 1/5/02,
> 1/24/02.

There were many partial projections all through as well. Although this door has closed, I have no regrets. . . . I feel extremely lucky for these life-changing experiences.

How did I know that I was not dreaming? The vibration/hiss happened most often in the morning just after waking but before stirring. We all believe in waking up. Everyone knows what it means to wake up. Before you open your eyes, your brain is back "on line"—you have returned; there are birds singing, sunshine filtering through your eyelids, and car engines drone in the neighborhood.

It was at this point where, if I remained motionless, the vibration/hiss would begin slowly, then amplify steadily. After a few moments it would reach a certain intensity and there would be a sensation of the physical body shedding off.

Trip Thirteen

The Native Americans

Notes 7/10/04: (1200 mg) (Into tape recorder.) Guardian spirits around me . . . they convey that they will protect me. They form a "wall" made up of themselves . . . surrounding me. They are Indian spirits! Some chieftain spirit came down and talked about the English people. He agreed that I was not as my grandfathers were. That I was of a different mindset than the earlier English . . . that he had known? There was communion and reconciliation. They welcomed me . . . the spirit guides. And we touched. (It was at this point that I began to chant . . . then sing, in tongues!)

So now in addition to the Buddhists, it was Indians . . . Native Americans, in the realms of the Dead acknowledging me. I had no preconceived ideas about spirit guides before I began this quest. In fact I didn't believe people who claimed they had guides. I didn't believe in contacting the Dead in any way.

The part to do with the tongues (yet another thing I scoffed at) happened as I was up, standing in my room. The sage became a thing of ultimate power. (How I understood this to be so I can't say.) Suddenly I began chanting/singing. . . . I don't know if these words are those of any Native tribes. (Maybe if there are any Native Americans reading this, they can let me know.) As I was singing, my jaw moving in a pattern as if something were singing through me, controlling my jaw, I reached for my tape recorder and got a few bars. Spelled phonetically it reads: "Bye ee ah chot chet yaa a yey yeea mo ah." This is *my* song. I can't explain how I know this.

A week after this encounter I was traveling in the mountains with the love of my life, Melissa. We were talking about omens when, out of the blue she said (to the Spirit), "Show me a sign!" At that instant we rounded a bend and lo! There was a sign tacked to a telephone pole: *Pow-Wow one mile.* We followed and found ourselves at a large Pow-Wow with many Native Americans dancing, playing tom-toms, etc. We sat with an elder named Grandmother River Bird who told us many things about her people the Leni Lenape.

Two weeks later we were at Lake Wallenpaupack in the Pocono mountains of Eastern Pennsylvania. We sat on a bench enjoying the view of the lake, me with the book *Prehistoric Cultures of Eastern Pennsylvania* by Jay F. Custer at my side, and what I thought might be a hide scraper wrought by a Native of yesteryear that I had found not long before. Melissa and I looked up at a couple approaching along the trail. Together we said: "Indians!"

Sure enough, two Native Americans, a woman in a plain brown dress and a man of about sixty, both with jewelry of turquoise and silver, had crossed our path. As they neared I held up the hide scraper, "Sir. Does that look like a hide scraper to you?"

The man smiled, a gleam in his eye. He looked at the book next to me and at the arrow head on a chain around my neck. He took the hide scraper from my hand and in a second said, "Nah that's not one."

His name is Joseph Greywolf and he lives in Honesdale, Pennsylvania. At the time of this writing Melissa and I have been invited to camp on his land (over a hundred acres) during a Pow-Wow with his many Native American friends. We will be the only "whites" present.

My friend who is a Seneca Indian told me that this encounter was no fluke. "You are on a path now. Don't question what appear to be coincidences any more."

And so I won't.

Afterthoughts

What do I really believe I have seen in the There? I wrestle with what I have experienced every day. In the bright daylight, weeks after an experience like the face-to-face interaction with an Other, a part of me wants to put it behind me and cast doubt on it all. But it is too late for such attempts by my ego to turn around the belief system that has arisen from my penetration into these "places." In fact beliefs in the solid-state yet spiritual realms one can witness in the closed-eye DXM trance have become Knowns for me.

These writings have been geared toward those like me, who have found themselves alone with the unspeakable. And anyway neuroscience or psychology is still in a position to lose credibility and funding, if such stories as encountering entities in nonphysical realms were pursued. Putting forth ideas dealing with psychedelic philosophy, in the end, must include more radical notions than the average person is willing to put much faith into. This can lead to isolation for those questing souls who have peered into Beyond . . . who bring back these true stories from the Source of

All. (Luckily, the internet has brought many otherwise remote travelers together for comparison of experience and general support. For the most part, I have found the people on Daniel Pinchbeck's *Breakingopenthehead.com* to be immensely helpful and understanding, when the lone tripper comes in with bent questions hardly syntactical. To his credit, Daniel Pinchbeck himself adds his thoughts—always profound and fascinatingly articulate—to a lot of the posts at the site.)

Speculation is bound to remain just that—speculative. However, careful observation must be getting near the truth somewhere along the lines of inquiry. What *is* on the Otherside must be a *this* or a *that*. Even if it is both—a This/That, as it would seem (the unwordable forfeit of the self, as has been covered— the questioner becoming the answer)—it is still a *something*.

Terence McKenna said in *The Archaic Revival* (page 69): "What we need now are the diaries of explorers. We need many diaries of many explorers so we can begin to get a feeling for the territory." He's absolutely right. Far-out notions can be whittled down over time, and a picture of the There will emerge. I am saying: we need to focus on navigation, specifically in closed-eye trances. I have discovered that what one can see in these states becomes somewhat routine. And routine is something psychedelic states do not lend themselves to (as far as I can see from the trip reports I have read). This is why I emphasize the closed-eye trance.

I have tested the waters on a few psychedelic Web sites with some of my findings with DXM, and to my surprise, some people would rather scoff at DXM without having ever tried it. (I hope DXM continues to be an underground psychedelic, even in the underground of psychedelics themselves.) I get the sense that those who profess "plant spirits" to inhabit ayahuasca or mushrooms, and show contempt for "man-made" chemicals, have somewhere deep within them an understanding of the realness of the DXM experience.

DXM is thrown in with ketamine by many psychonauts. The trips may be similar but ketamine is short acting and for that reason, in my opinion, addictive—always leaving the tripper chasing the Point of Entry. Many psychedelic searchers profess to be on a spiritual quest but will avert their gaze, so to speak, at certain critical times during psychedelic states. The implications of ego-loss, for example, isn't taken seriously—we are not what we seem and no one wants that to be so. In the end most don't really want to take the mask off of the Wizard of Oz. If really knowing what's back There isn't one's thing, the psychedelic experience, I suppose, will be whatever one chooses to believe it to be. My approach has been absolutely spiritual despite its appearance to some. Exploration with psychedelics must be the exploration of death in the final outcome. If it is not, the quest is full of what one would like it to be or mean.

Bibliography

Alphern, Henry. *An Outline History of Philosophy*. Toronto: Forum House, 1969.

Behe, Michael J. *Darwin's Black Box*. New York: Simon & Schuster, 1996.

Berkeley, George. *A Treatise Concerning the Principles of Human Knowledge*. 1710; reprint, Cambridge, Mass.: Hackett Publishing, 1982.

Briggs, John, and F. David Peat. *Turbulent Mirror*. New York: Harper & Row, 1989.

Chilton Pearce, Joseph. *The Crack in the Cosmic Egg*. Rochester, Vt.: Park Street Press, 2002.

Czerner, Thomas B. *What Makes You Tick? The Brain in Plain English*. New York: John Wiley & Son Inc., 2001.

Eliade, Mircea. *Shamanism: Archaic Techniques of Ecstasy*. New York: Arkana, 1964.

Goswami, Amit. *The Self-Aware Universe*. New York: Putnam's Sons, 1993.

Gould, Stephen Jay. *Wonderful Life*. New York: W. W. Norton & Co., 1989.

Hayes, Charles. *Tripping*. New York: Penguin Compass, 2000.

McKenna, Terence. *The Archaic Revival.* San Francisco, Calif.: HarperSanFrancisco, 1991.

Monroe, Robert. *Journeys out of the Body.* Garden City, N.Y.: Doubleday, 1971.

Narby, Jeremy. *The Cosmic Serpent.* New York: Jeremy P. Tarcher/Putnam, 1998.

Pinchbeck, Daniel. *Breaking Open the Head.* New York: Broadway, 2002.

Rajneesh, Bhagwan Shree. *Meditation: The Art of Ecstasy.* New York: Harper & Row, 1976.

Ramachandran, V. S., and Sandra Blakeslee. *Phantoms in the Brain.* New York: Harper Perennial, 1999.

Schroeder, Gerald. *The Science of God.* New York: Free Press, 1997.

Sheldrake, Rupert, Terence McKenna, and Ralph Abraham. *Chaos, Creativity, and Cosmic Consciousness.* Rochester, Vt.: Park Street Press, 2001.

Shulgin, Alexander, and Ann Shulgin. *PiHKAL.* Berkeley, Calif.: Transformation Press, 1991.

Strassman, Rick. *DMT: The Spirit Molecule.* Rochester, Vt. Park Street Press, 2001.

Books of Related Interest

DMT: The Spirit Molecule
A Doctor's Revolutionary Research into the Biology
of Near-Death and Mystical Experiences
by Rick Strassman, M.D.

LSD, Spirituality, and the Creative Process
Based on the Groundbreaking Research of Oscar Janiger, M.D.
by Marlene Dobkin de Rios, Ph.D., and Oscar Janiger, M.D.

Moksha
Aldous Huxley's Classic Writings on
Psychedelics and the Visionary Experience
by Aldous Huxley
Edited by Michael Horowitz and Cynthia Palmer

The Sacred Mushroom Seeker
Tributes to R. Gordon Wasson by Terence McKenna,
Joan Halifax, Peter T. Furst,
Albert Hofmann, Richard Evans Schultes, and Others
Edited by Thomas J. Riedlinger

The Encyclopedia of Psychoactive Plants
Ethnopharmacology and Its Applications
by Christian Rätsch

Plants of the Gods
Their Sacred, Healing, and Hallucinogenic Powers
by Richard Evans Schultes, Albert Hofmann, and Christian Rätsch

Magic Mushrooms in Religion and Alchemy
by Clark Heinrich

The Mystery of Manna
The Psychedelic Sacrament of the Bible
by Dan Merkur, Ph.D.

Inner Traditions • Bear & Company
P.O. Box 388 • Rochester, VT 05767
1-800-246-8648
www.InnerTraditions.com
Or contact your local bookseller